the Poor Man's Picasso

ink drawings

&

Coloring Book

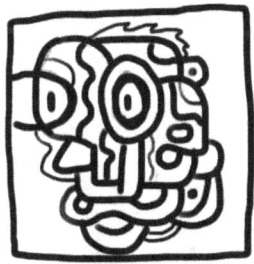

© 2015

James Sasso

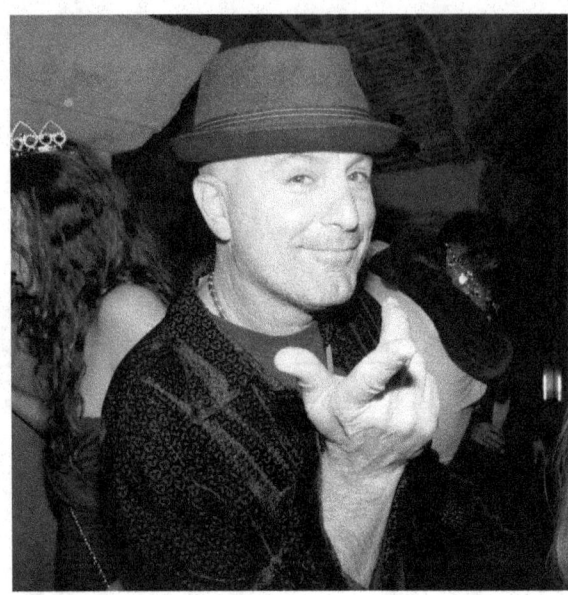
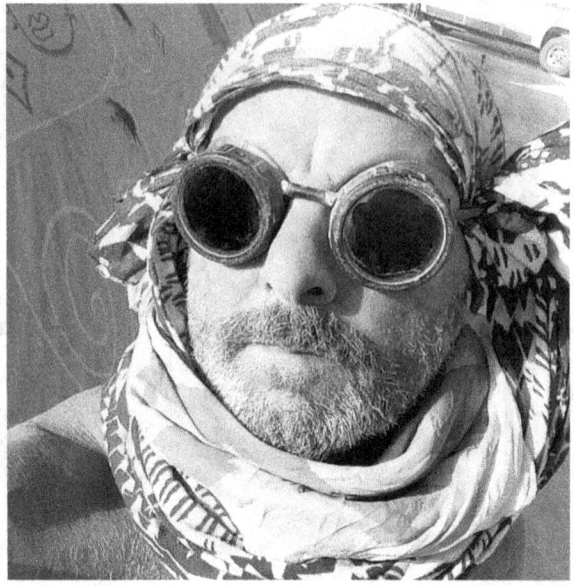

About the artist:
James Sasso is an artist, yogi and nature lover. He eats and cooks all natural foods. Sasso has also written and illustrated 3 children's books dealing with our environment. He hopes to animate the concept as well as many others he is creating. For more information or to contact him, please go to his web links as follows..,
His personal site is ARTTOGO.com
Instagram - Sasso the cat
facebook -   JamesSasso1
Twitter -- Space_junkers

Acknowledgements

Thank you Peggy.

THE POOR MAN'S PICASSO
A collection of ink drawings and coloring book

ISBN - 13:978-1519102058

ISBN - 10:1519102054

INSTRUCTIONS

If you wish to add colors then colored pencils work well and certain colored pens also.

Making art can often be a theraputic type experience because the participant gets lost in the simplicity of the endeavor.

Some say that time and thoughts are the same thing so pay only close attention to the process of adding color to the black and white images. Focus on the task of adding your flair to the experience as there is no right or wrong. The images will come to life with color.

ONLY THE MAN WHO CAN RELAX IS ABLE TO CREATE, AND IDEAS REACH HIS MIND LIKE LIGHTNING.

-CICERO

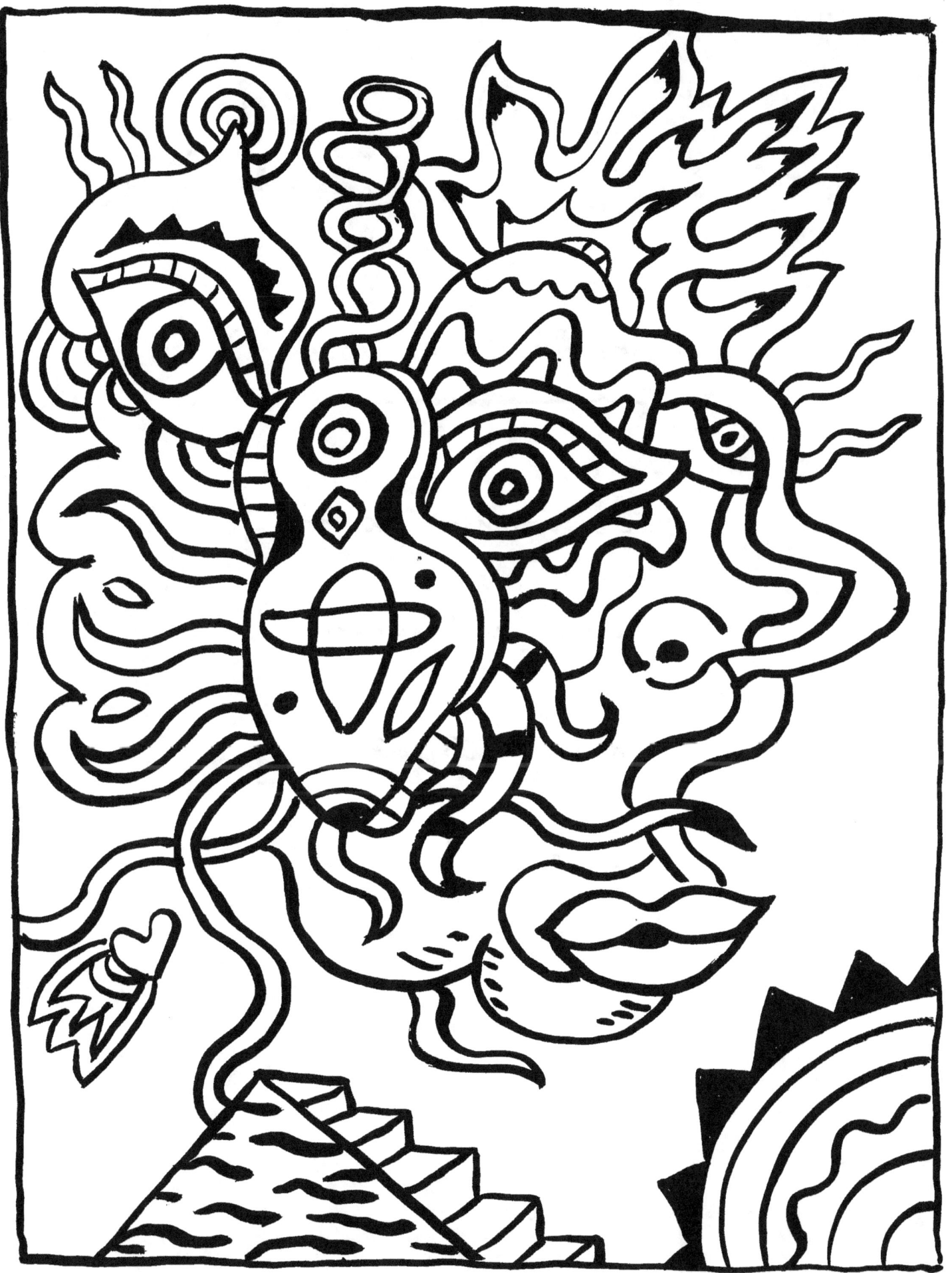

the Poor Man's Picasso

The poor man's Picasso

he never eats nachos.

He never eats nothing

at all.

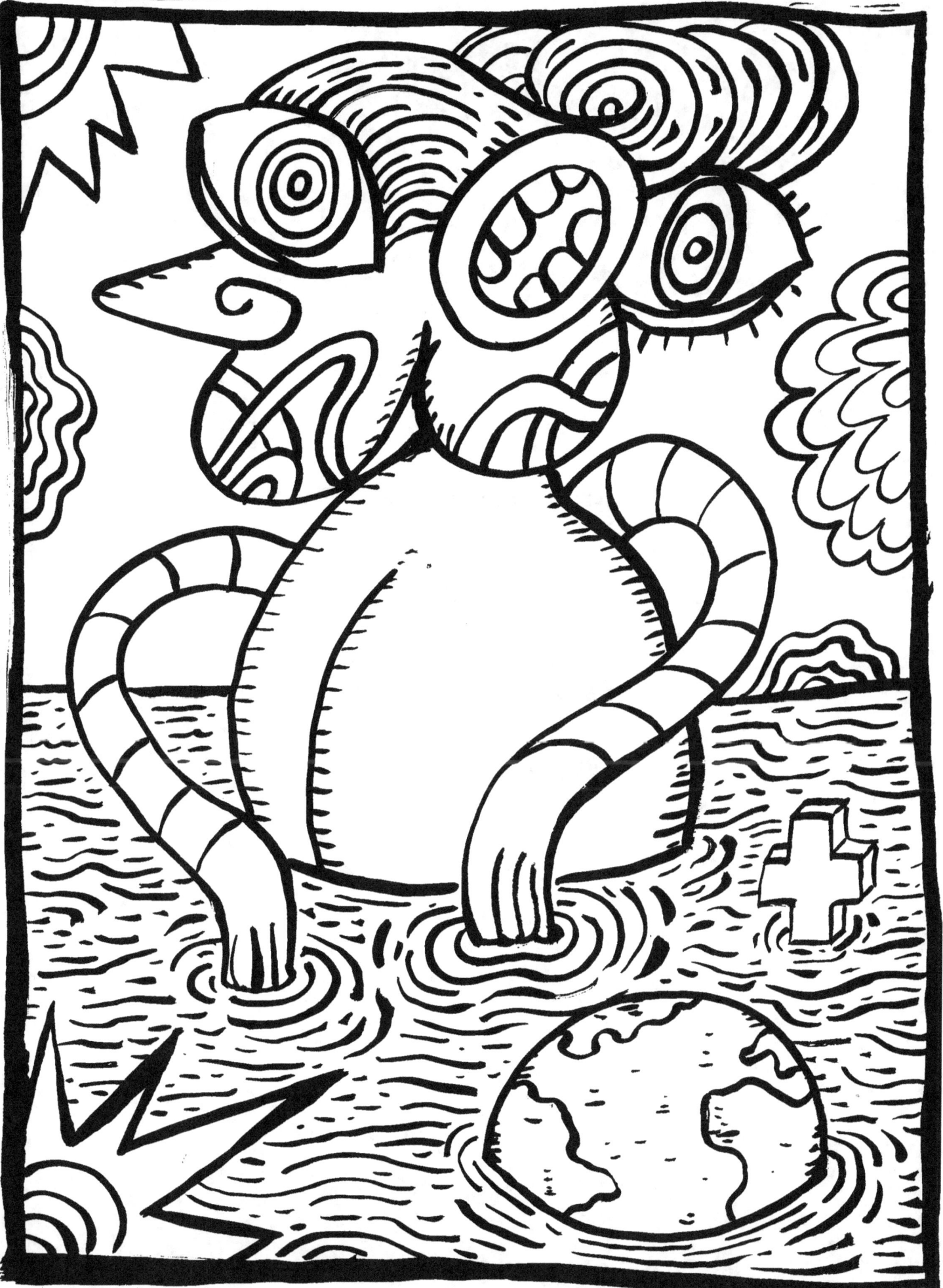

He lives in a dream.

Or so it may seem.

He lives in his head

after all.

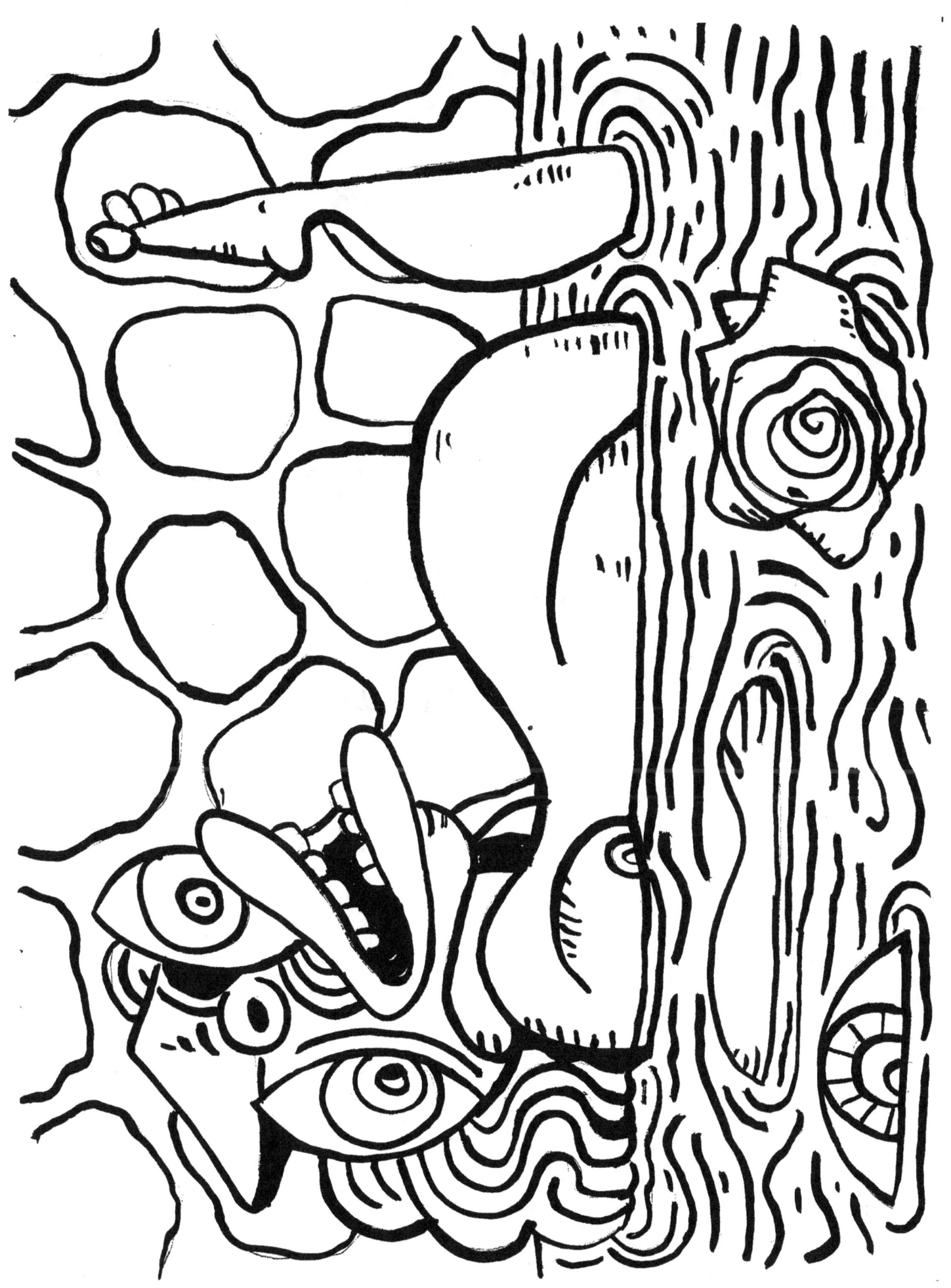

Oh why in this life?

He questions his strife.

There is nothing to do

but paint.

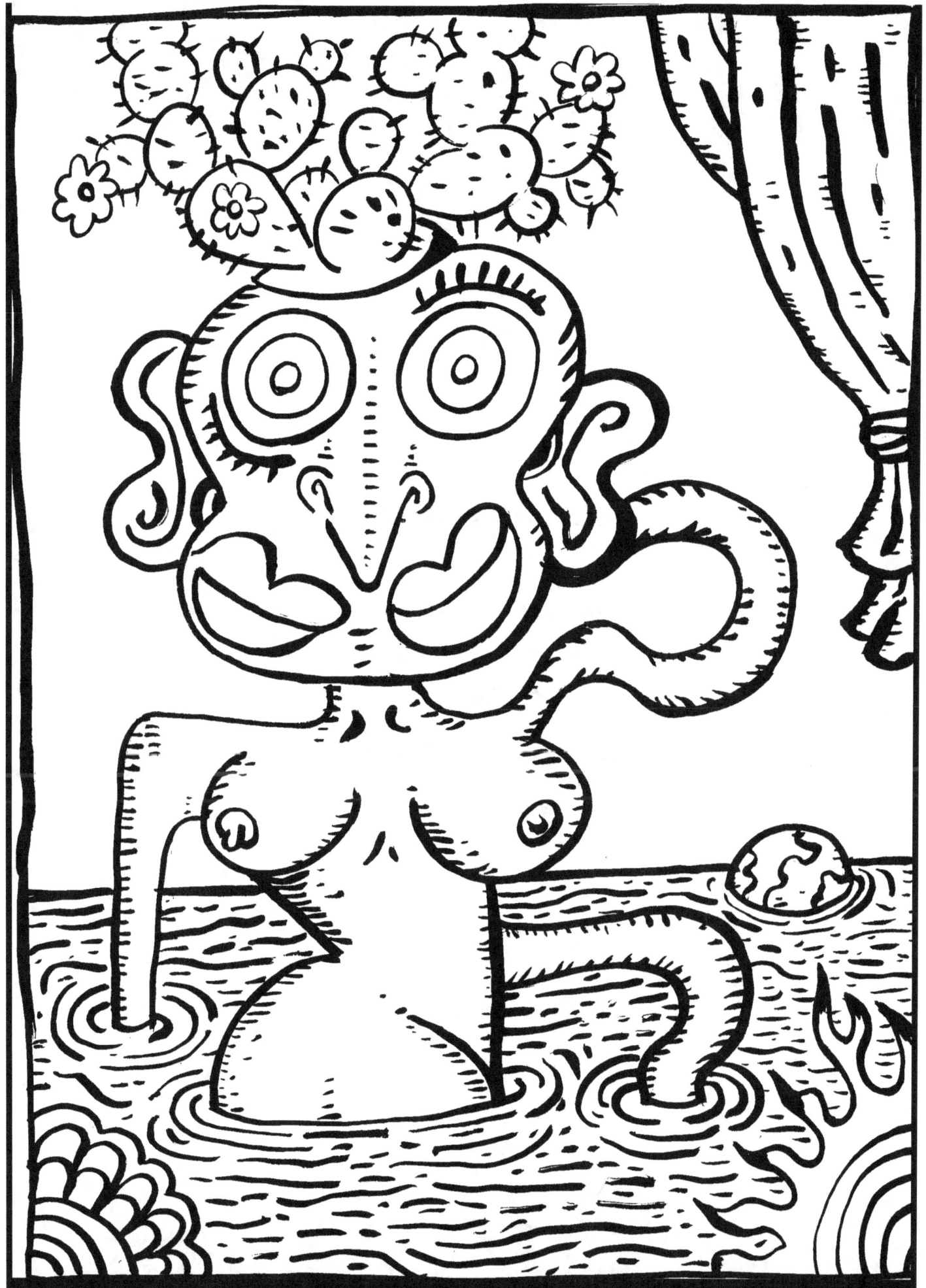

the piss poor Picasso,

does not live in Paris,

or hang
with the culture
elite.

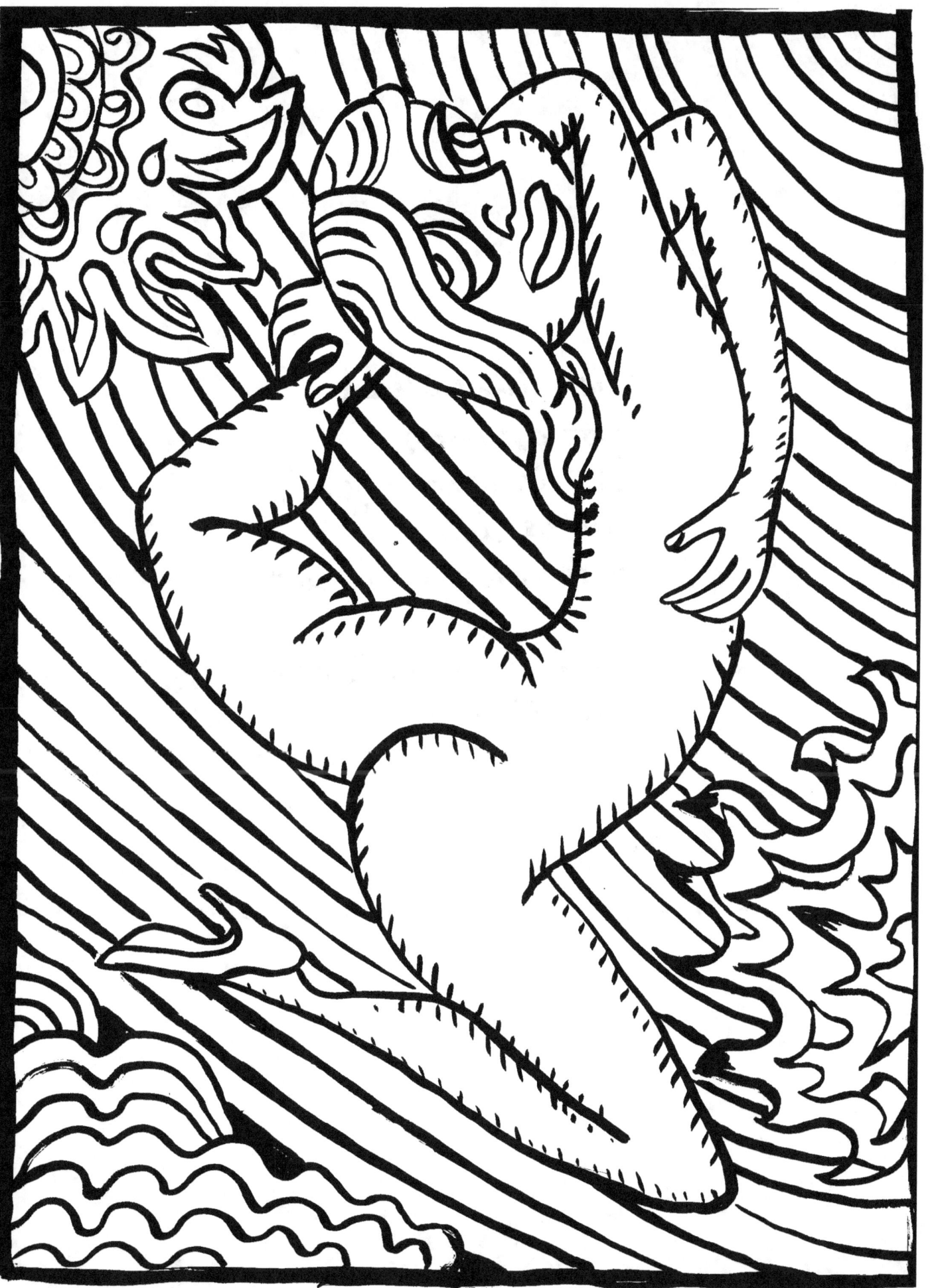

No damsels,
No dames,
fat women or girls.
No ladies
nor hookers with curls.

the poor man's Picasso,
eats rice
every day,
with his matzo.
This is the life
of the poor man's Picasso.

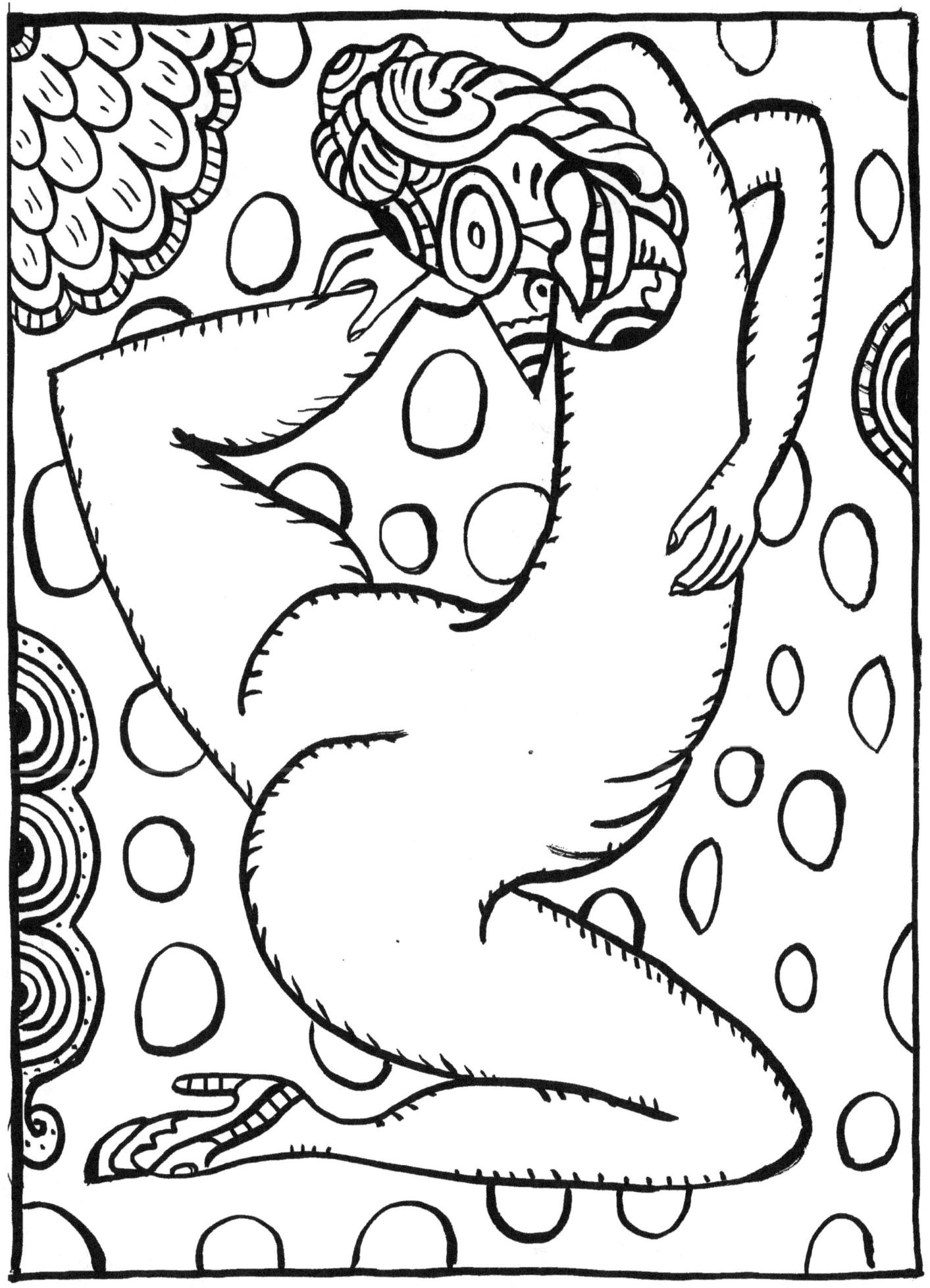

He drinks all the wine
in all
a good time.

The art is all here

you will see.

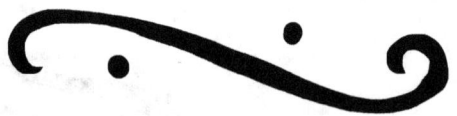

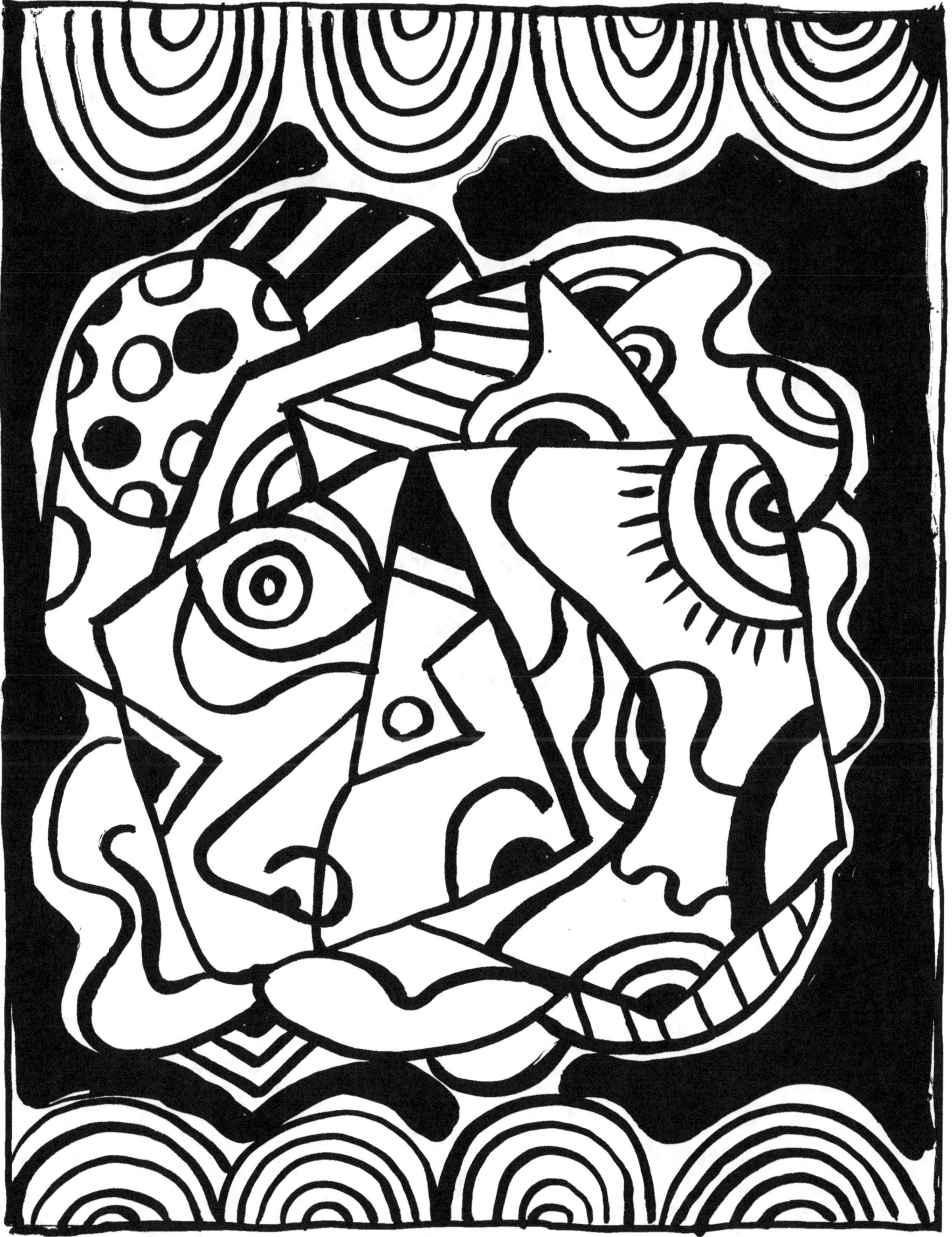

"WE ALL KNOW THAT ART IS NOT TRUTH. ART IS A LIE THAT MAKES US REALIZE TRUTH OR AT LEAST THE TRUTH THAT IS GIVEN US TO UNDERSTAND. THE ARTIST MUST KNOW THE MANNER WHEREBY TO CONVINCE OTHERS OF THE TRUTHFULLNESS OF HIS LIES."

— PABLO PICASSO

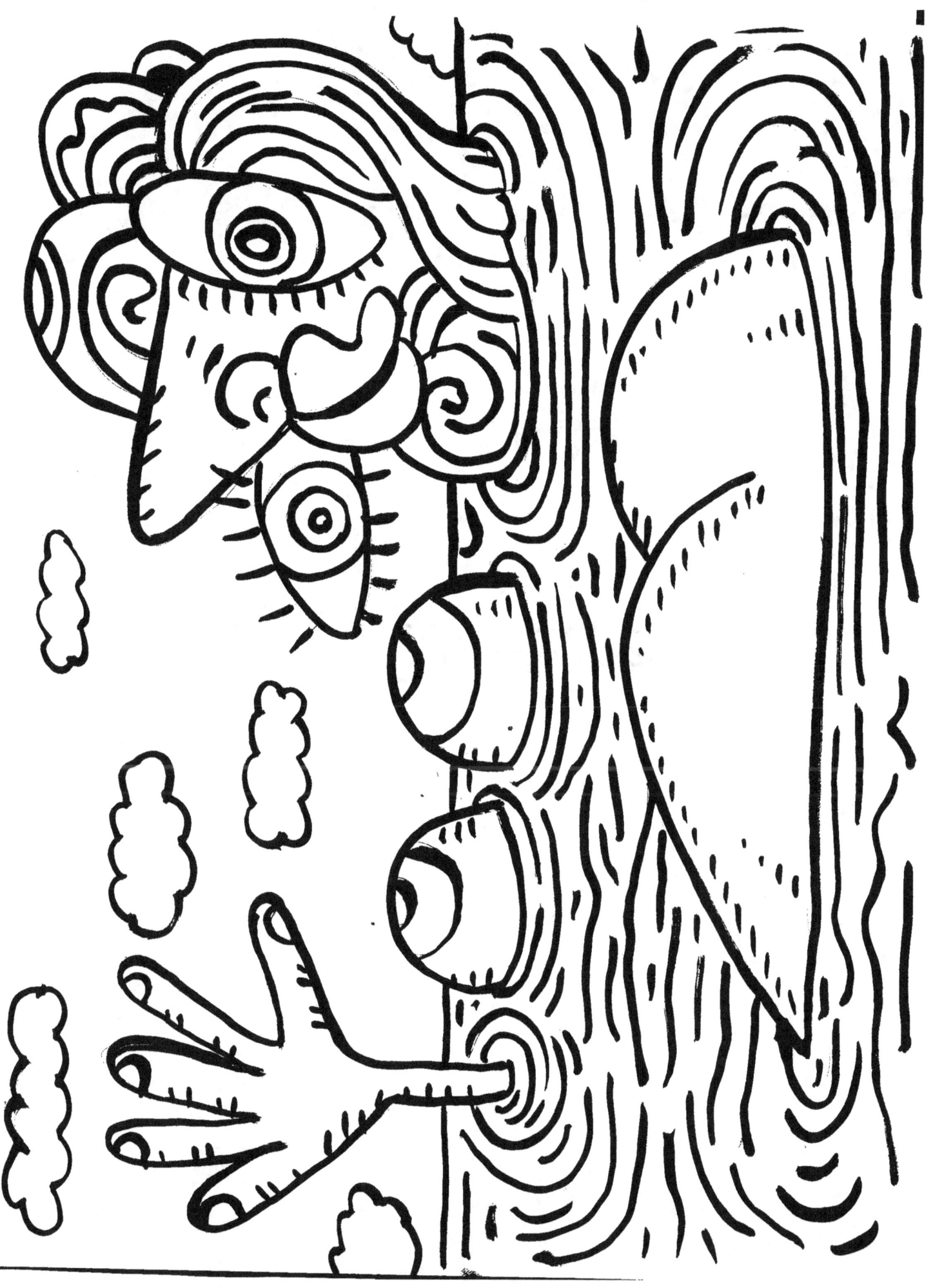

Vision is the art of seeing what is invisible.

— Jonathan Swift

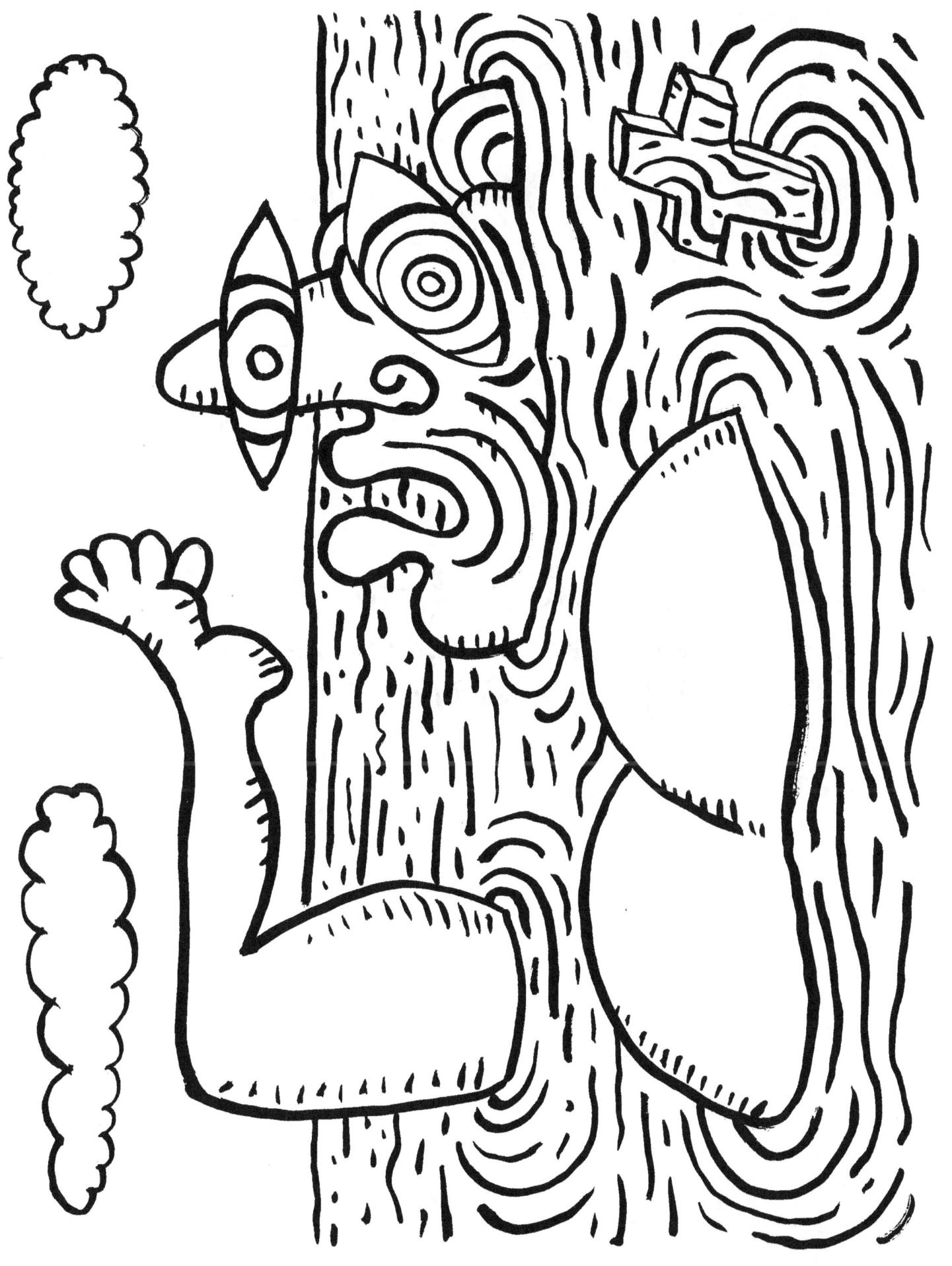

The highest form of
research is essentially
play. — EINSTEIN

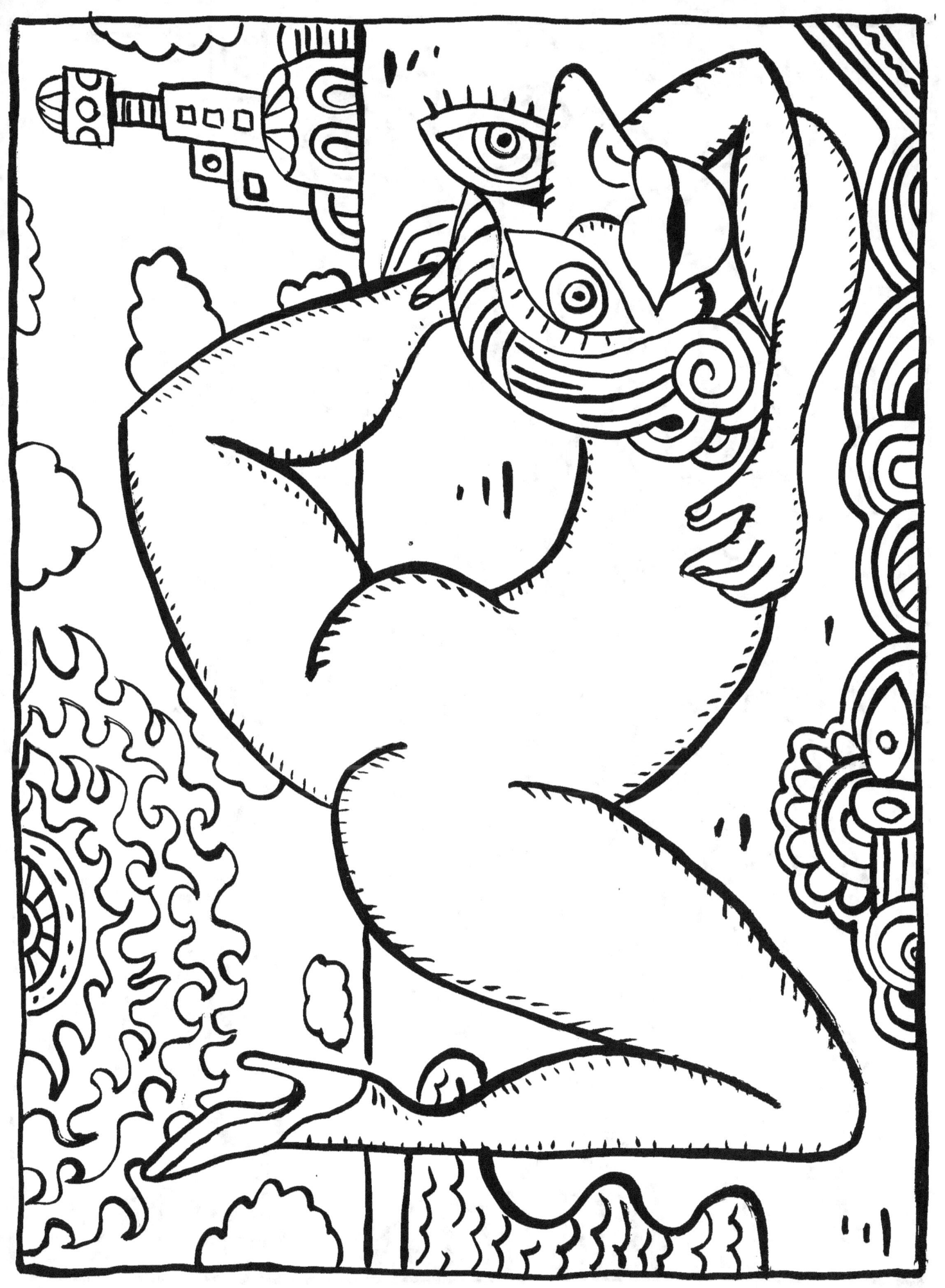

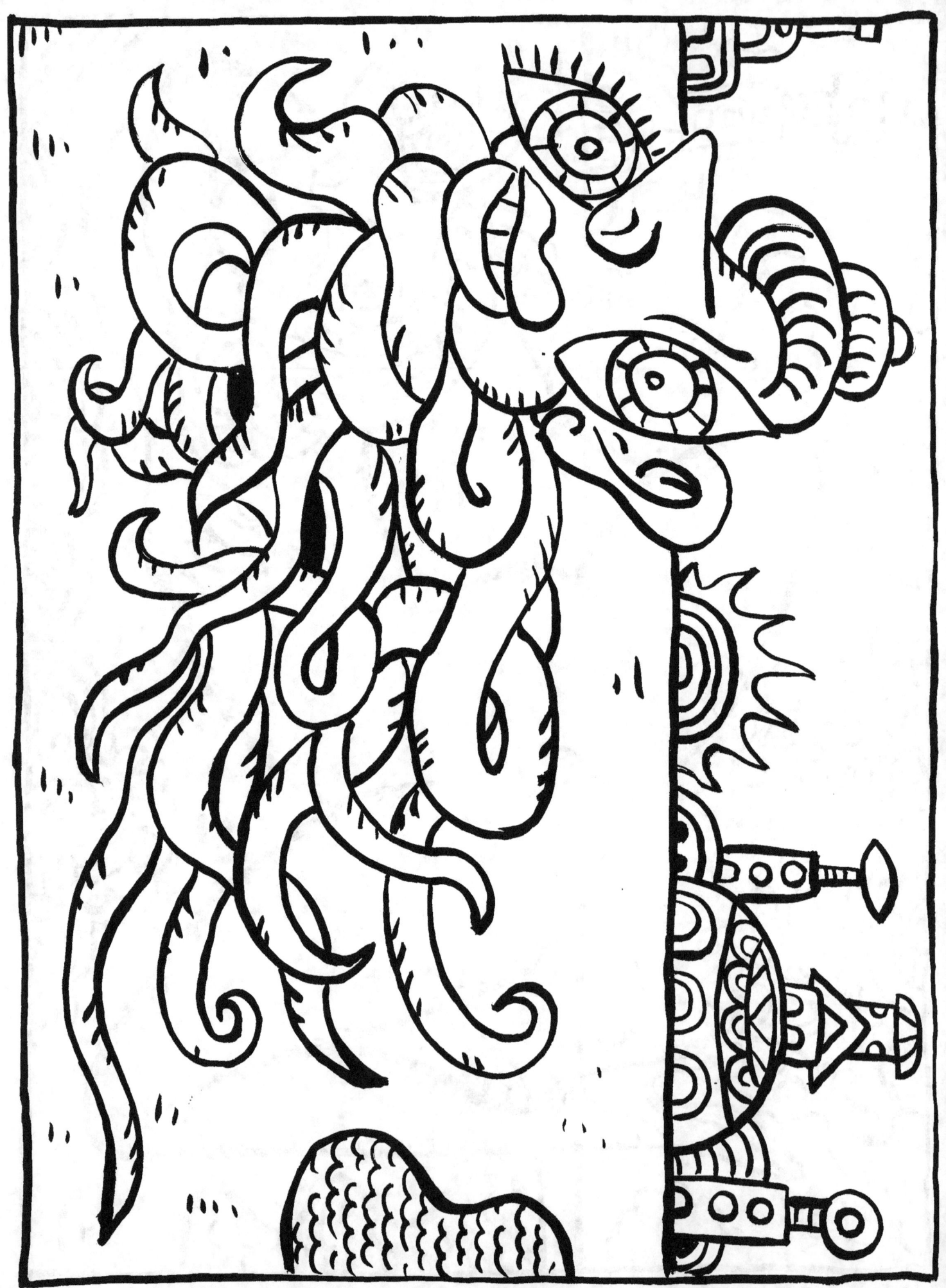

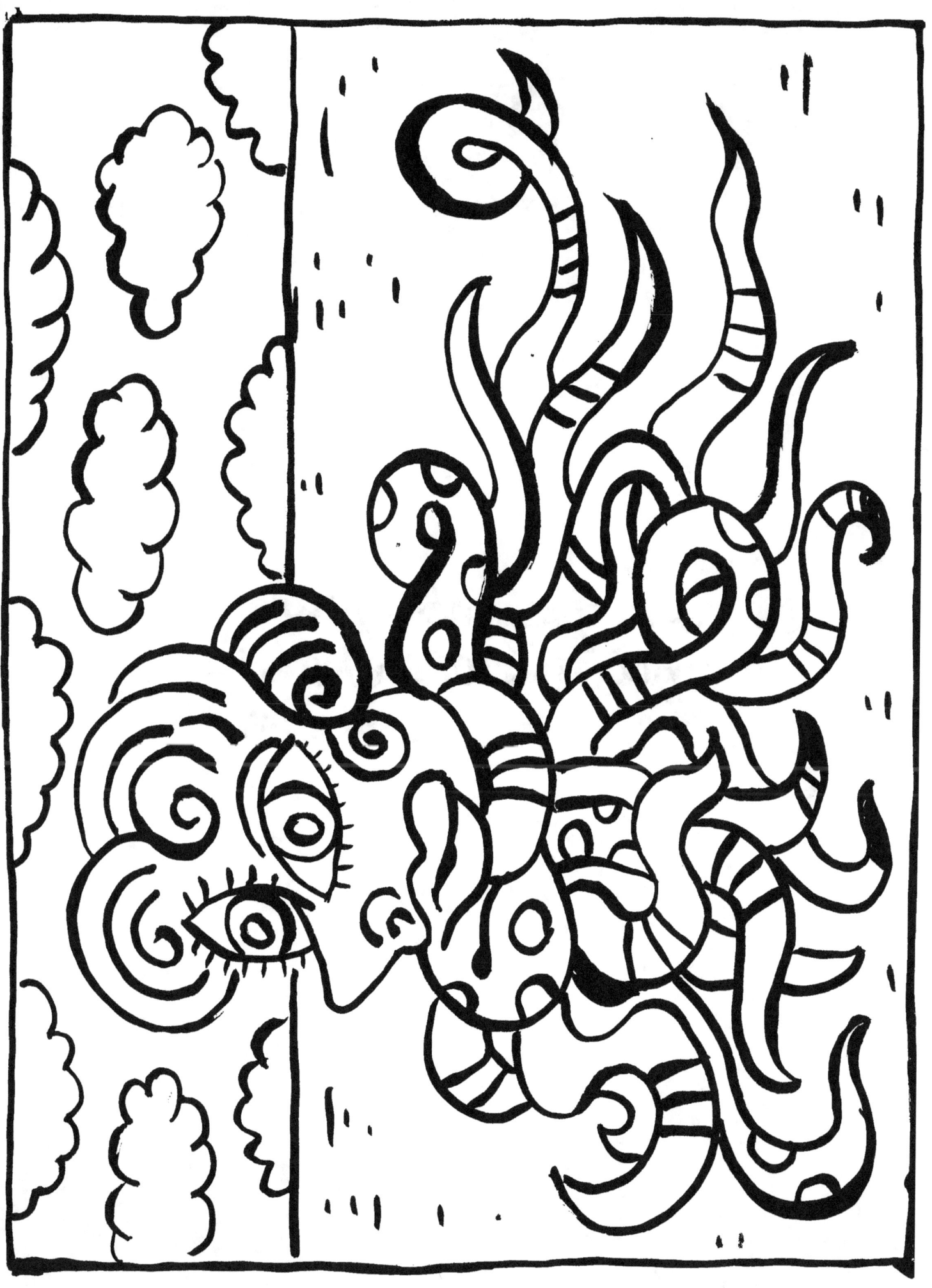

Do you not know
that you are Gods.

                    — John 10:34

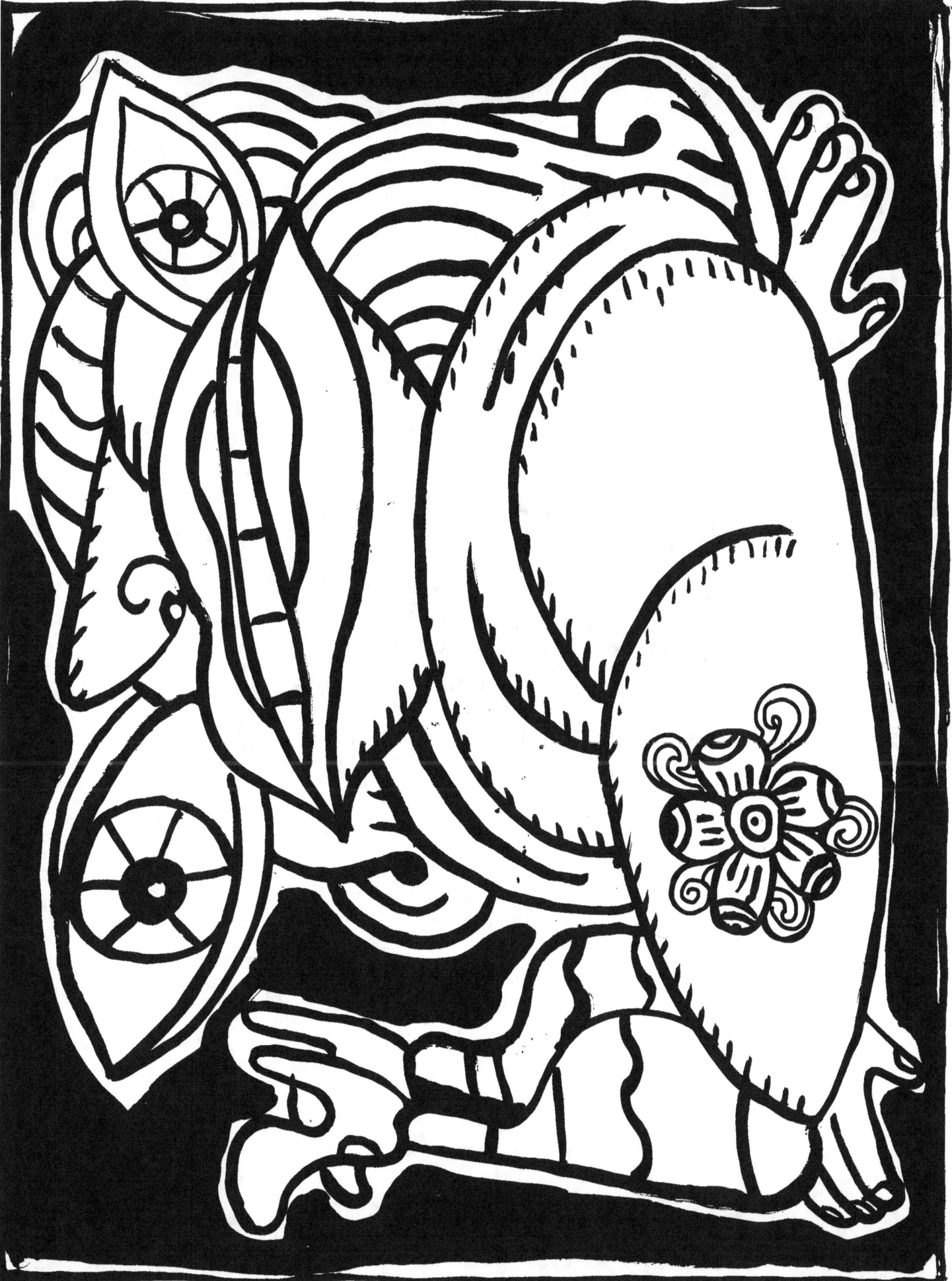

EDUCATION IS AN
ADMIRABLE THING.
BUT IT IS WELL TO
REMEMBER FROM
TIME TO TIME THAT
NOTHING THAT IS WORTH
KNOWING CAN BE TAUGHT.
— OSCAR
WILDE

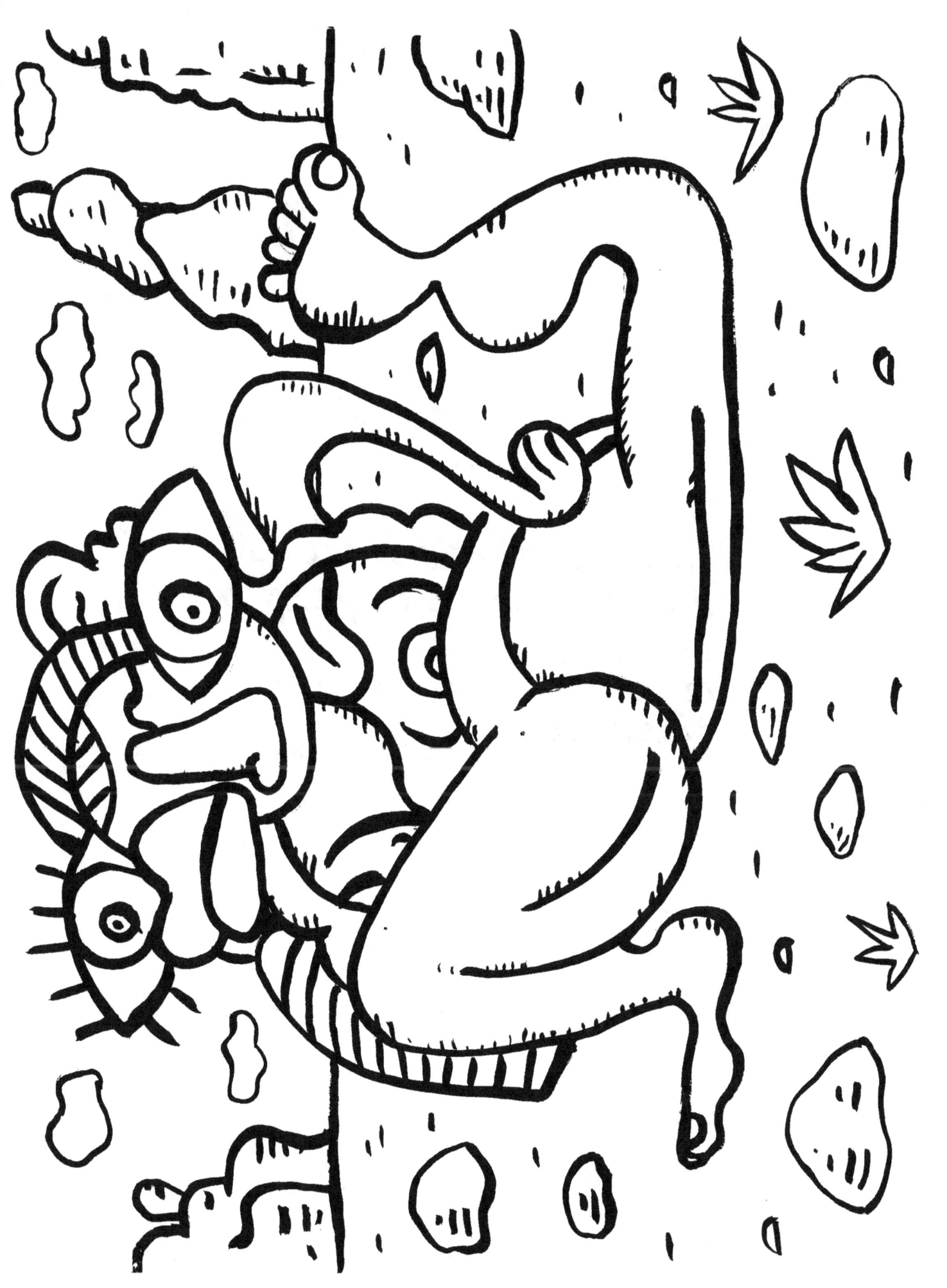

Man's perceptions are not bound by organs of perception; He perceives more than sense (tho' ever so acute) can discover. — William Blake

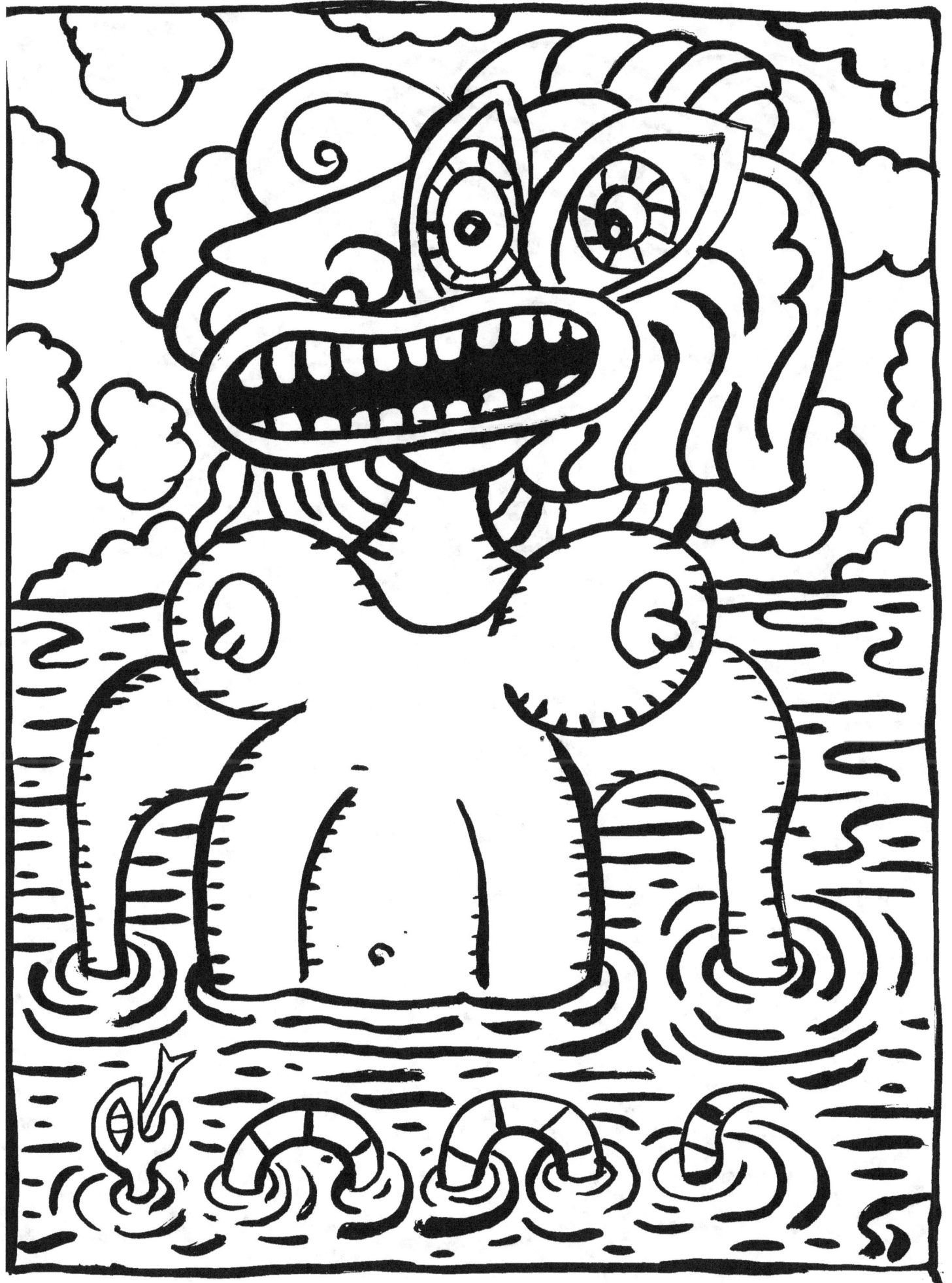

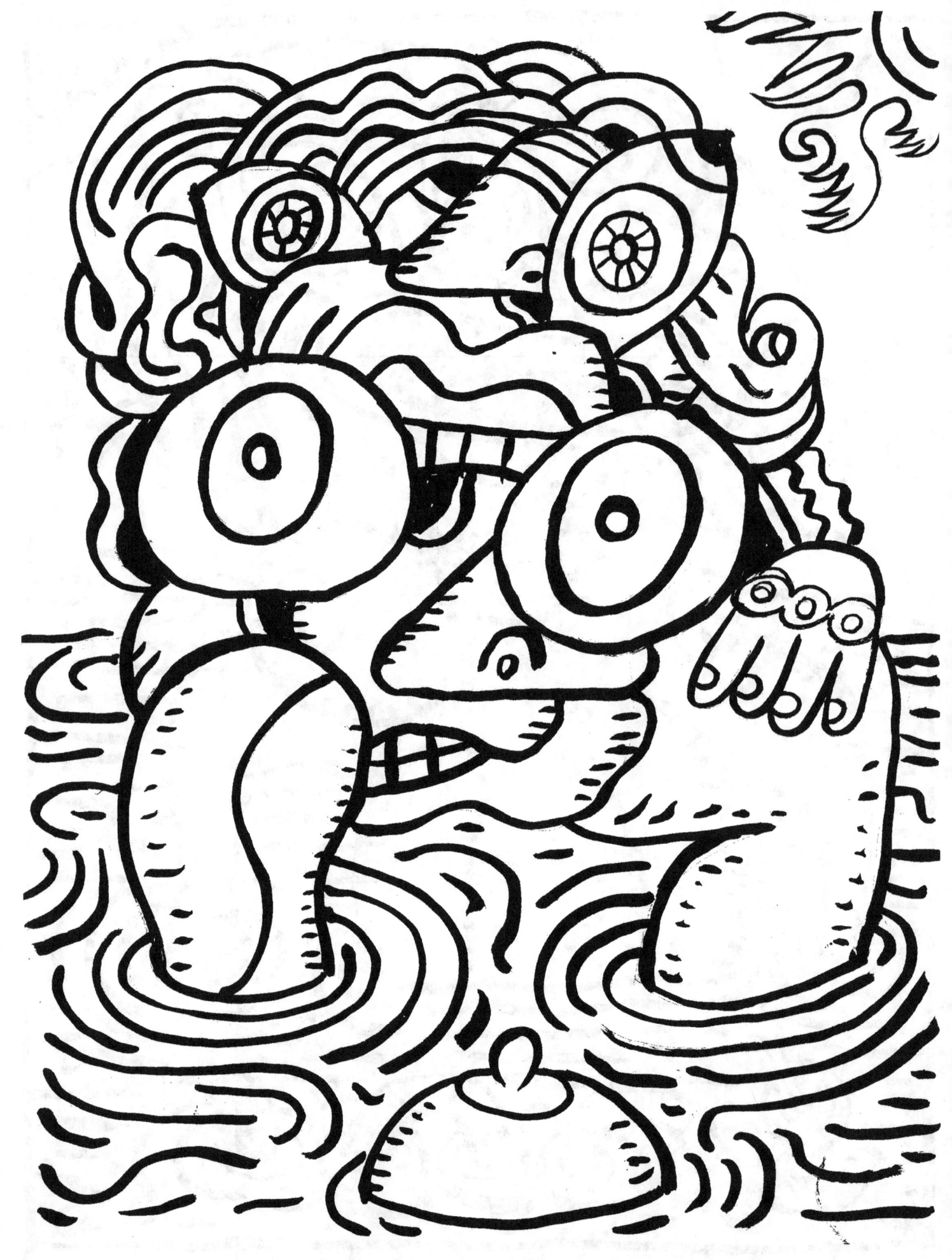

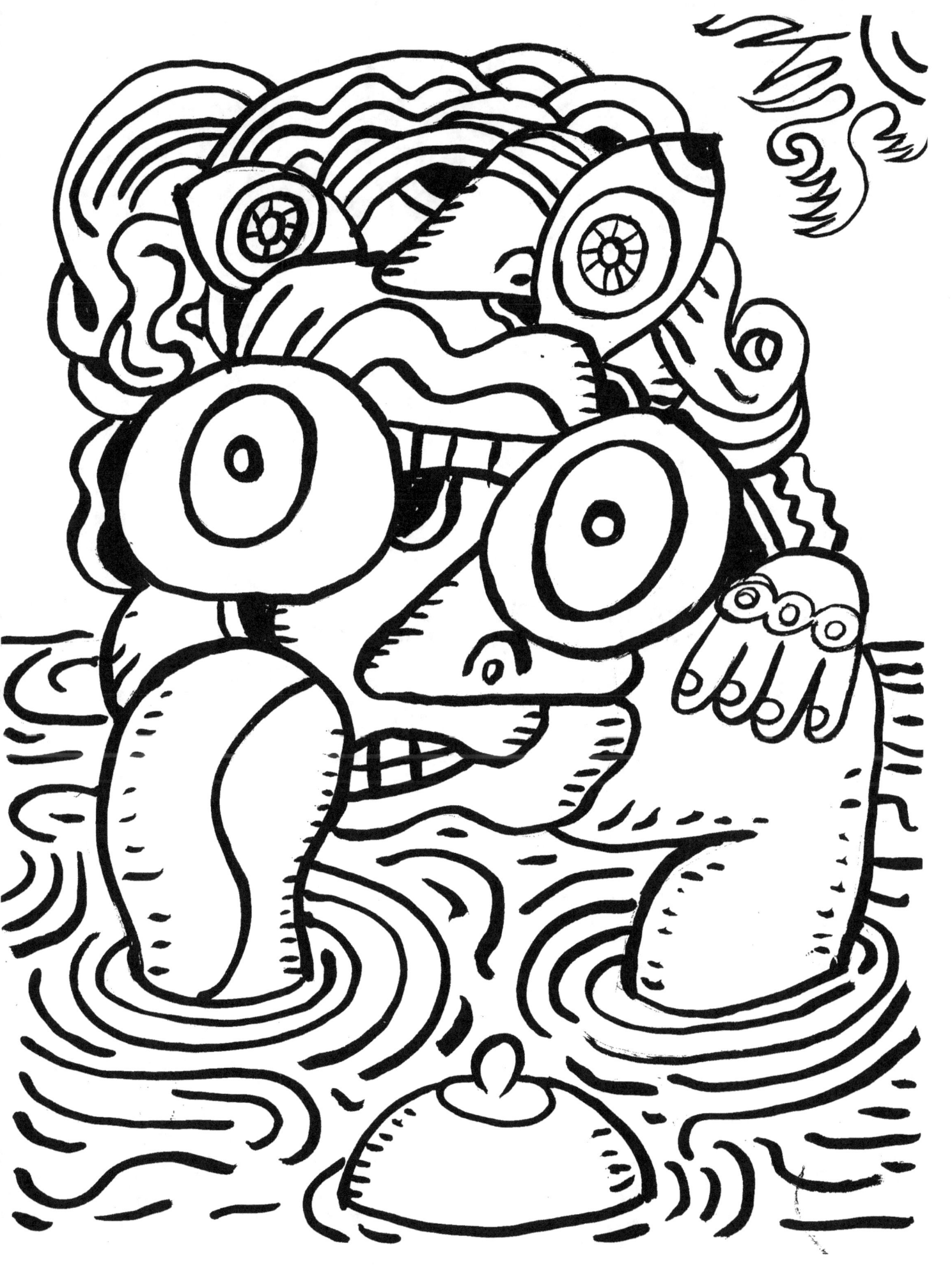

MUSIC IN THE SOUL CAN BE
HEARD BY THE UNIVERSE.

— LAO TZU

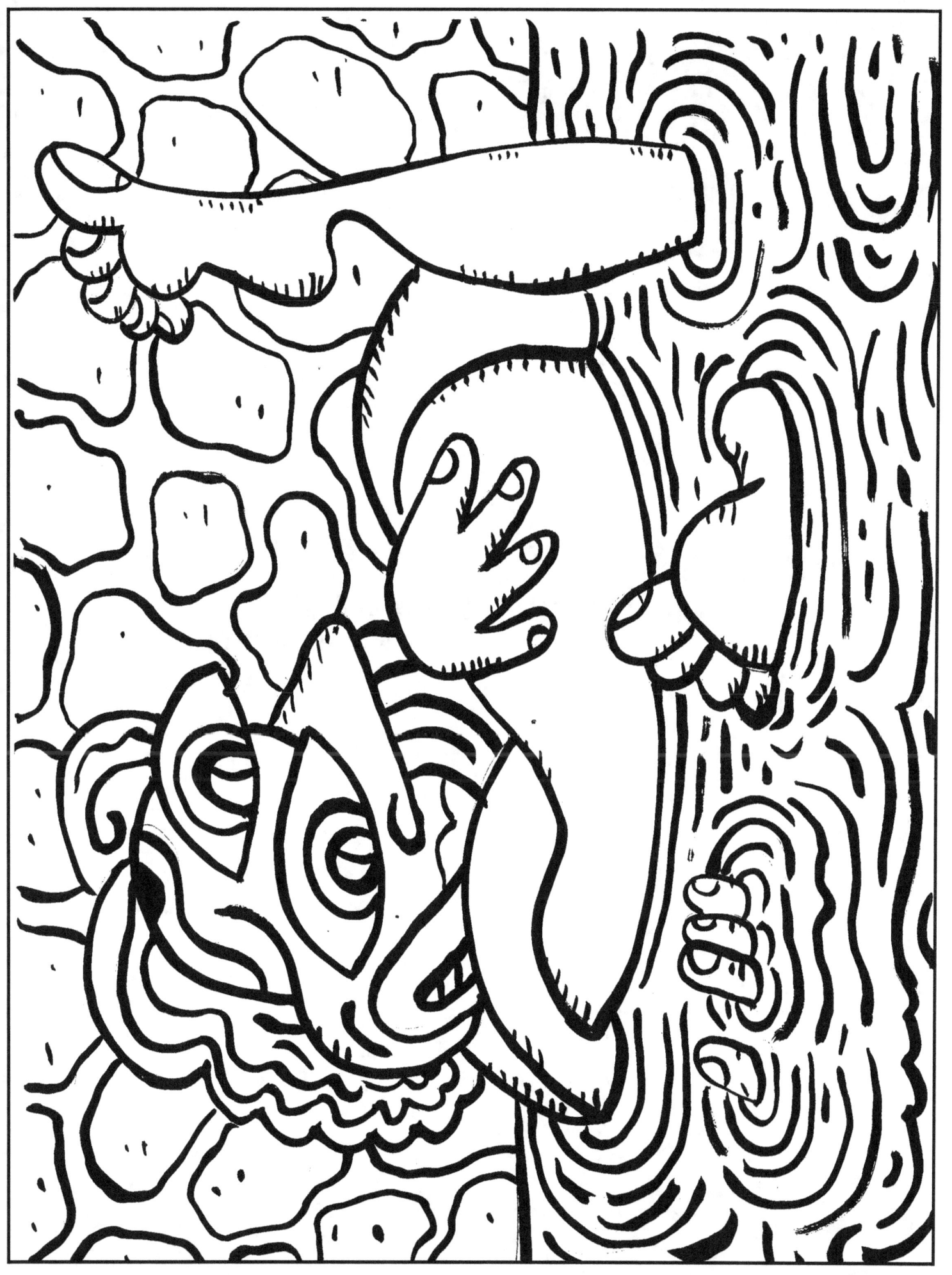

Your HEART IS EVERYWHERE.
                    ~ PRAJNAPARAMITA

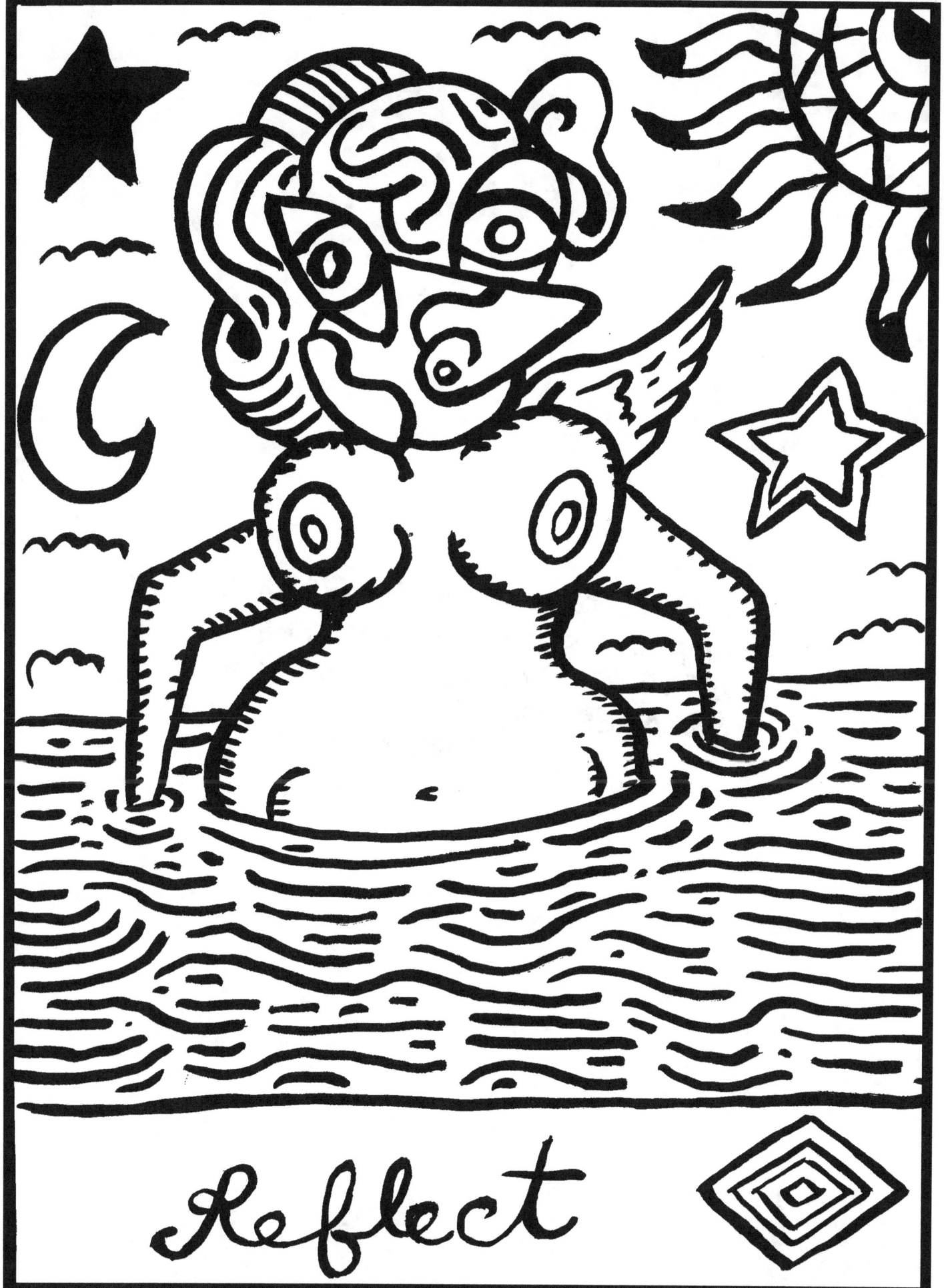

Reflect

AND GOD CALLS THINGS THAT ARE NOT SEEN AS THOU THEY WERE SEEN AND THE UNSEEN BECOMES SEEN.

ROMANS 4:17

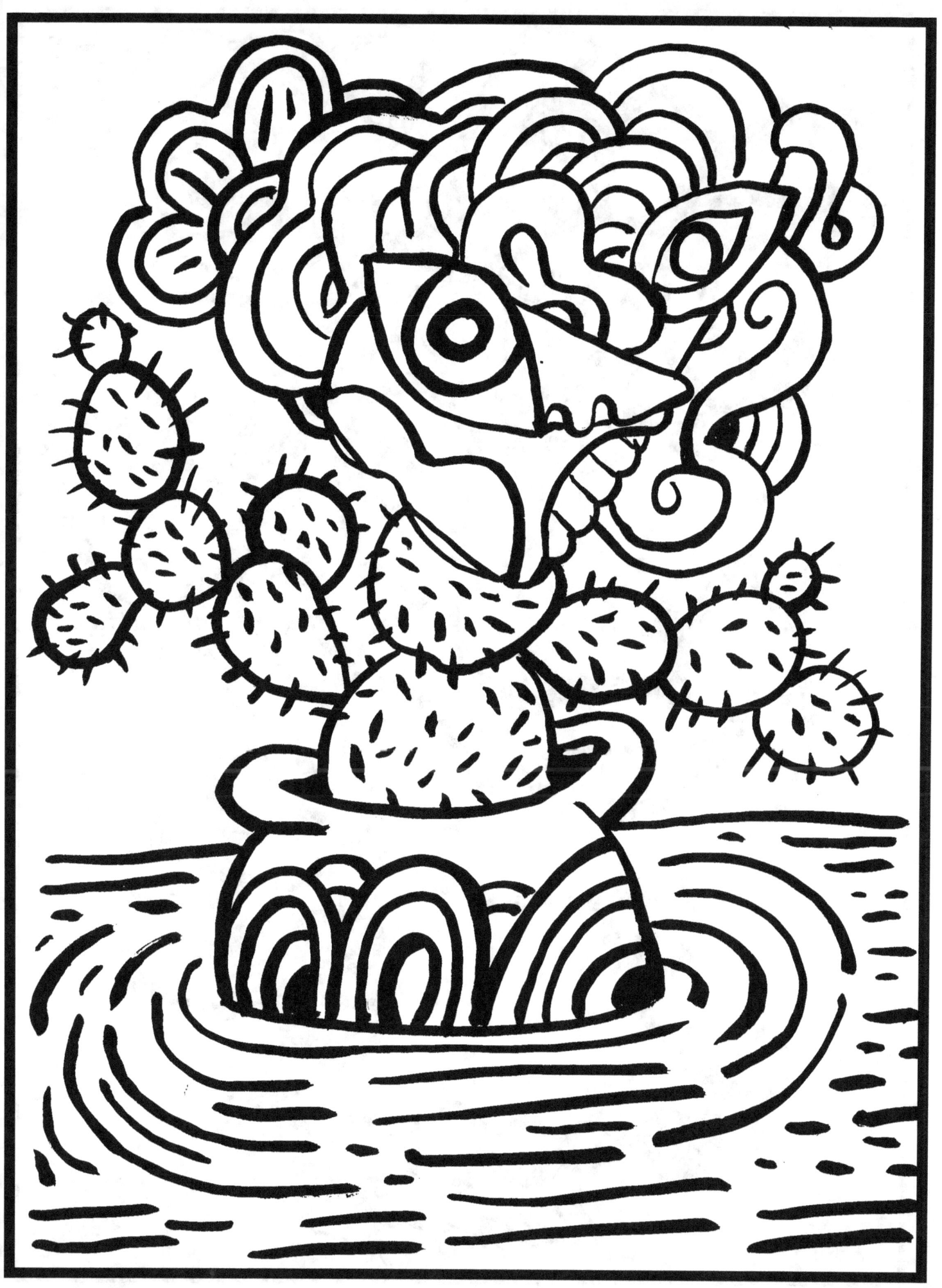

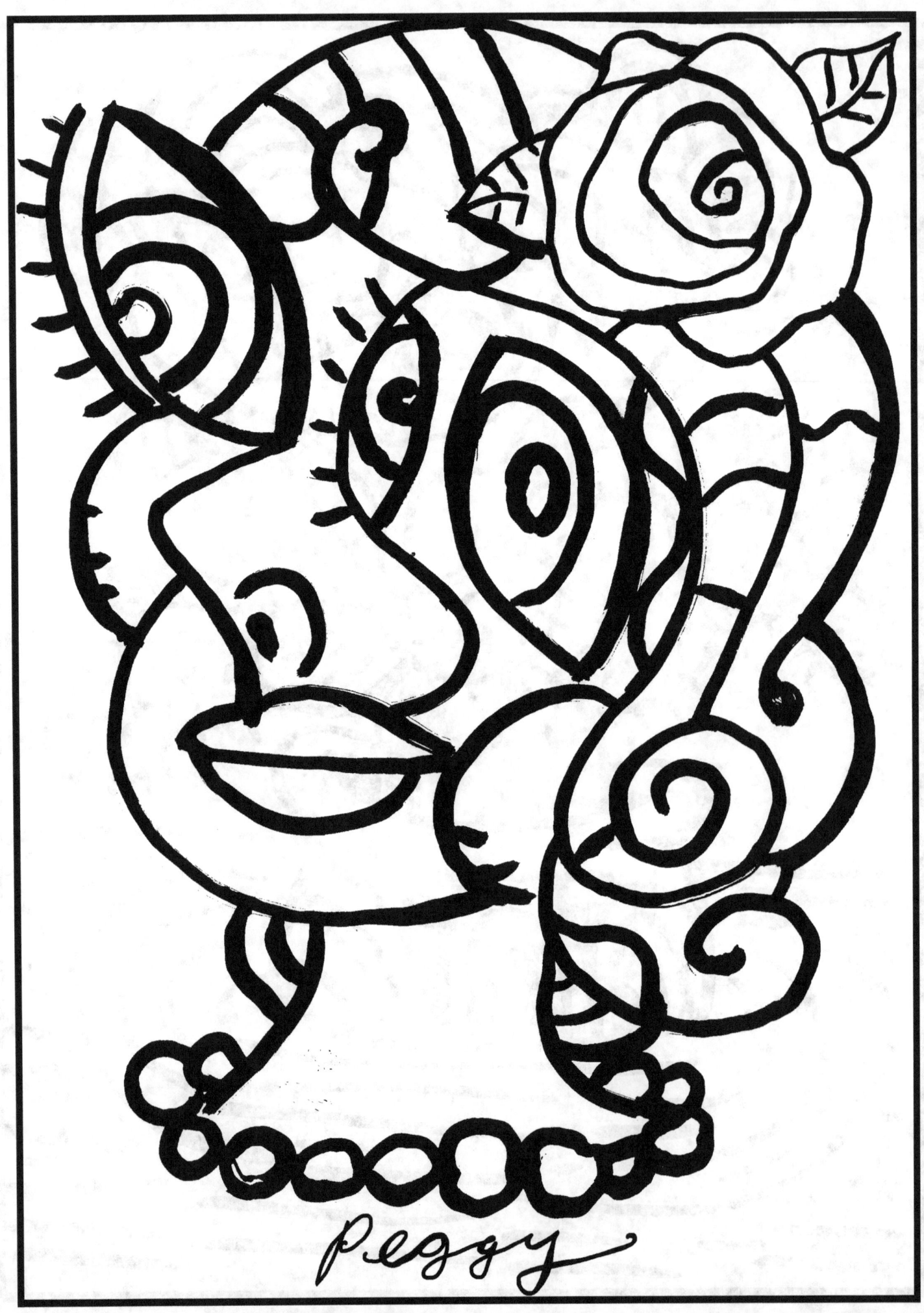

Peggy

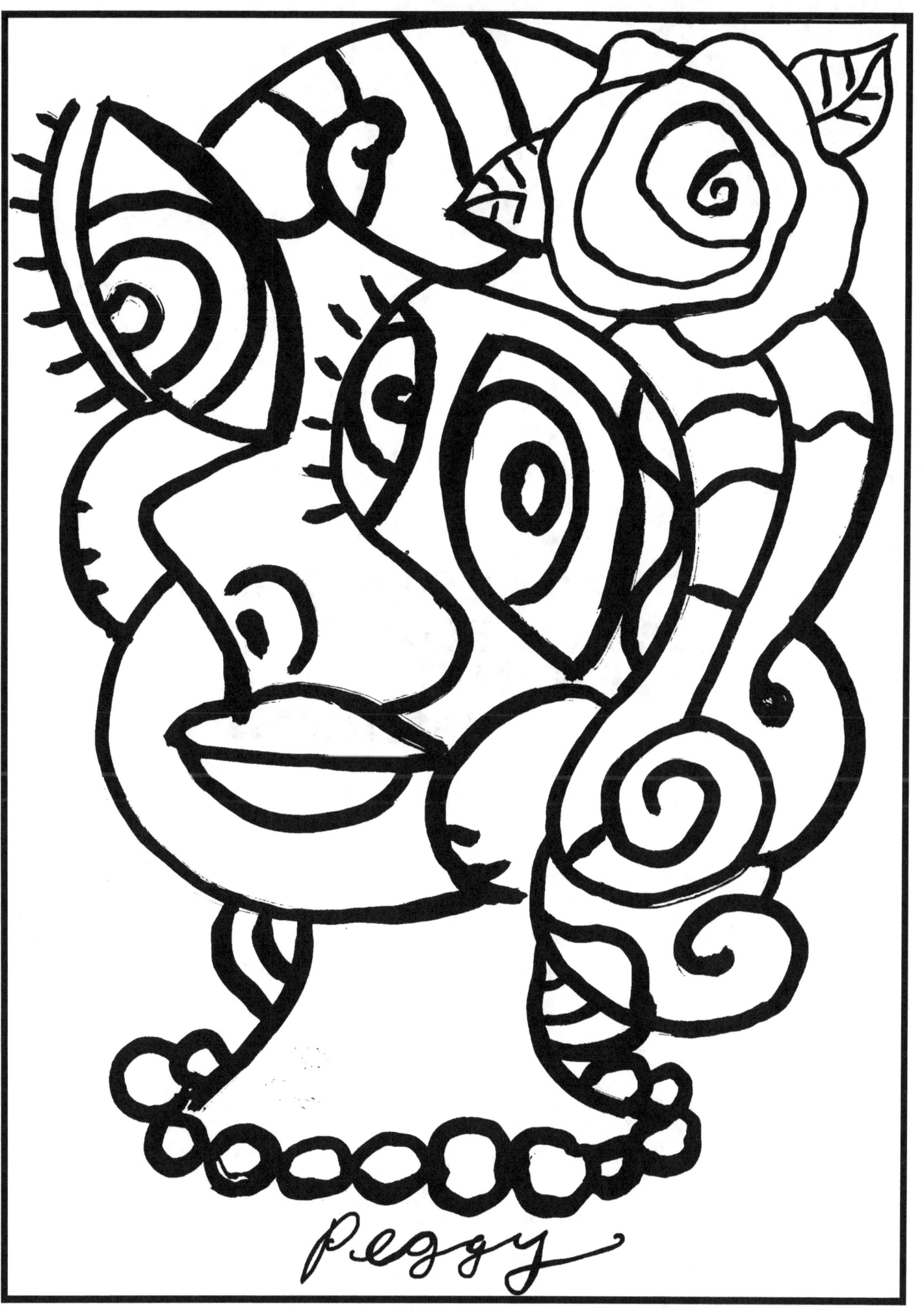

IF WE GIVE SPIRITS A
FORM, WE BECOME
INDEPENDENT.
                    —PABLO PICASSO

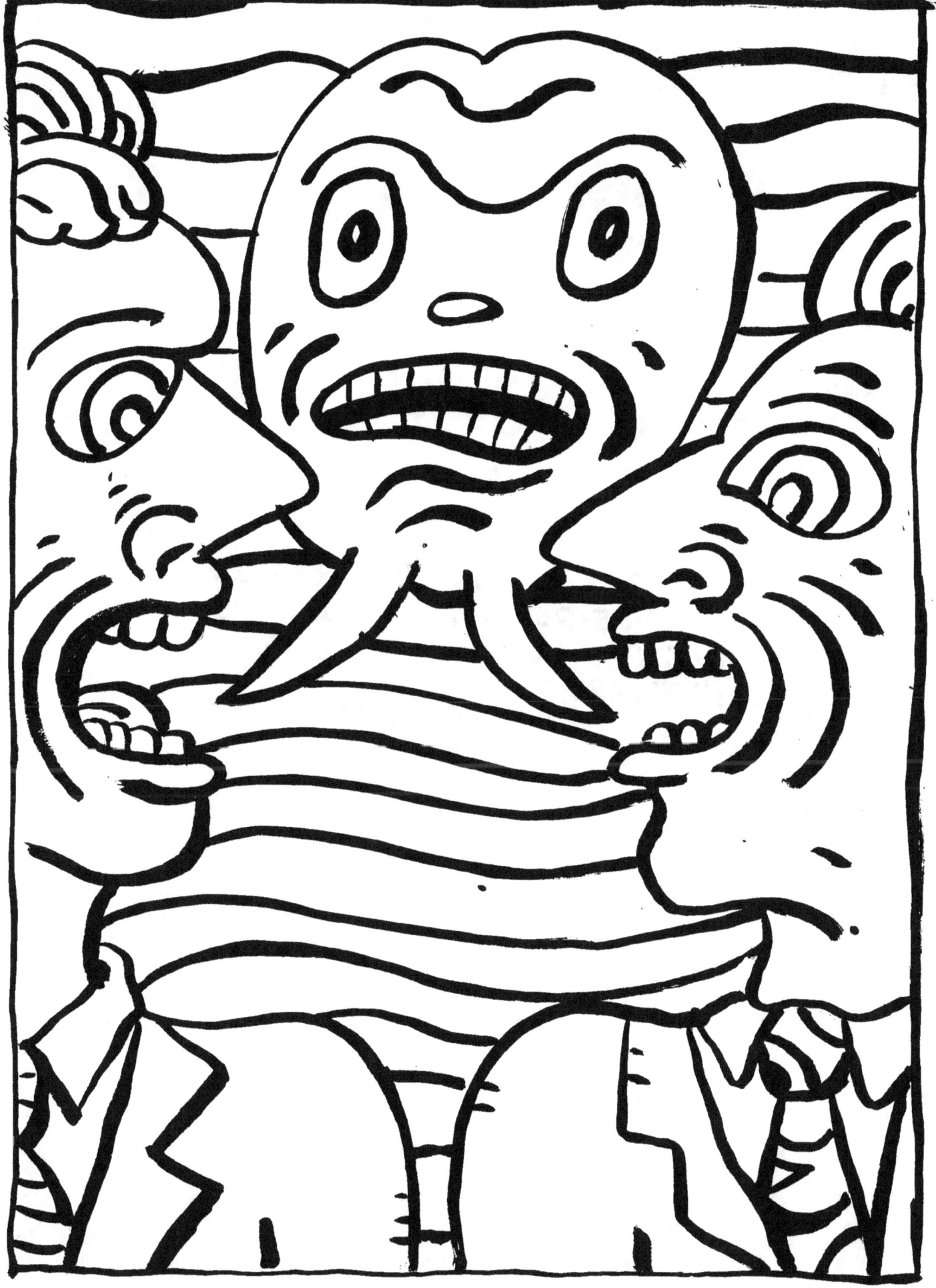

ENERGY CANNOT BE CREATED
OR DESTROYED, IT CAN ONLY BE
CHANGED FROM ONE FORM TO
ANOTHER.
                    - ALBERT EINSTEIN

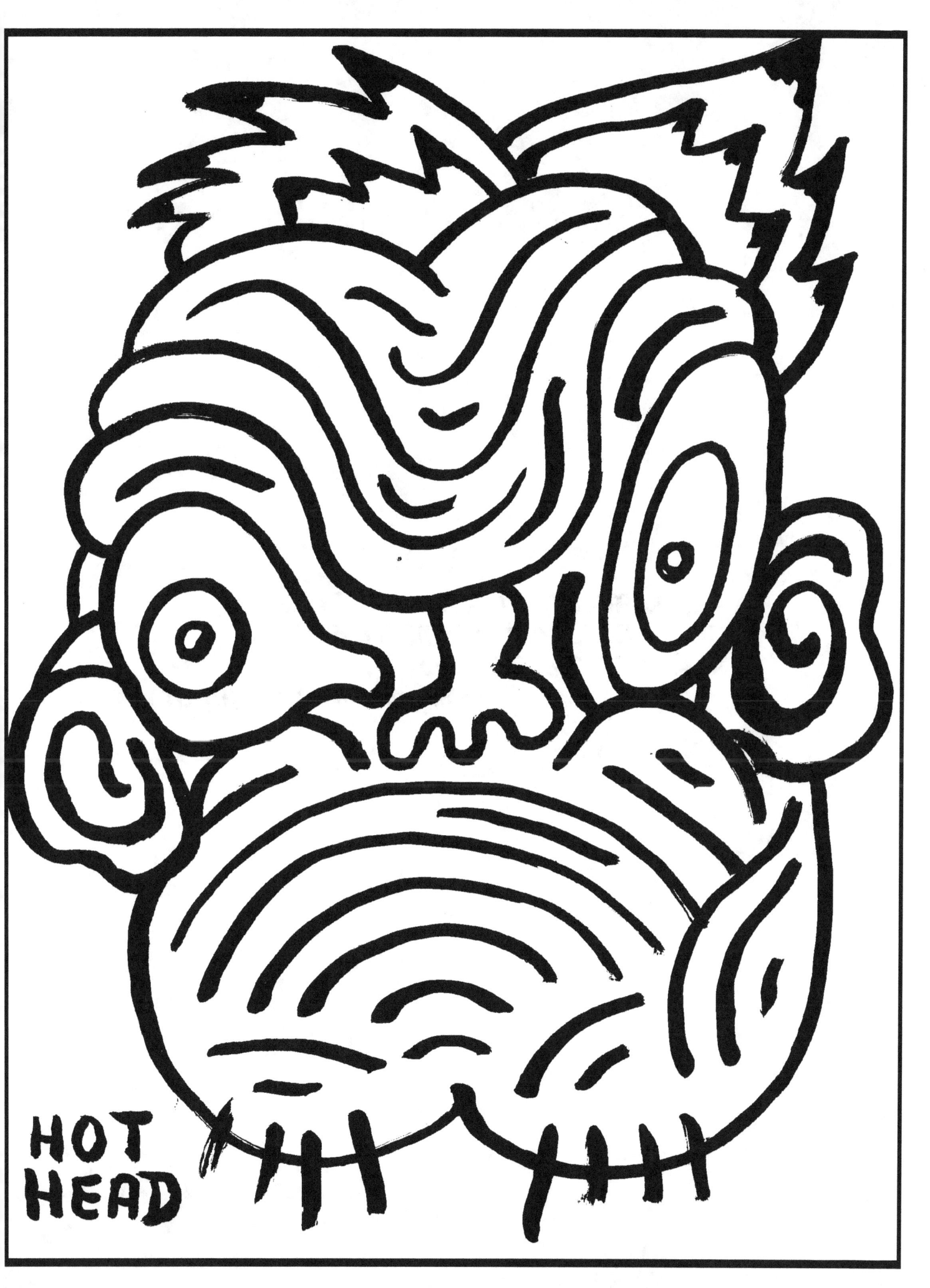

HOT
HEAD

ALL NATURAL LAWS OF THE
UNIVERSE, ATTRIBUTE THEIR
SUCCESS TO PATIENCE.
                    —THE DIAMOND SUTRA

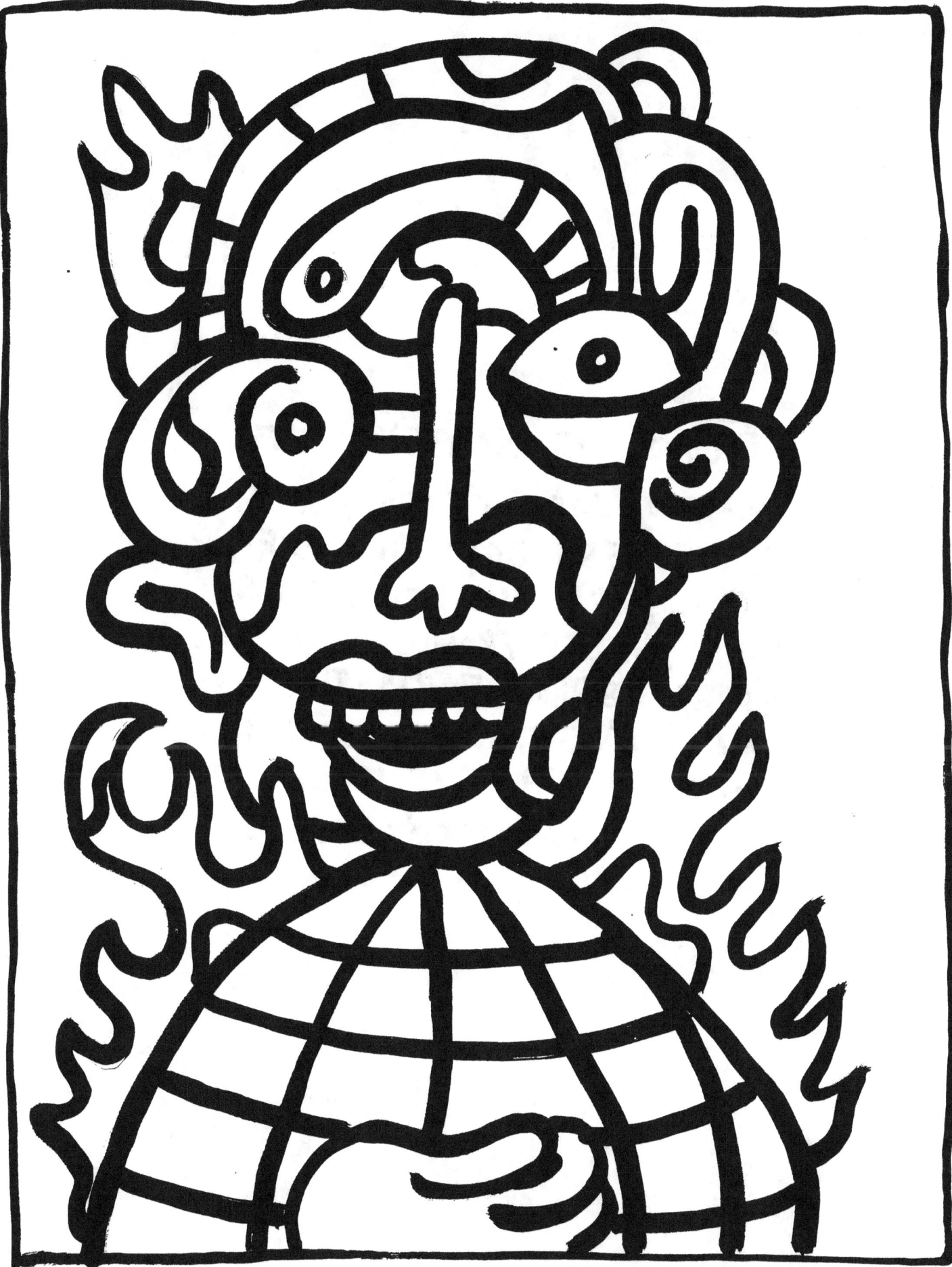

FORM IS EMPTY, YET
EMPTINESS IS ALSO FORM.
EMPTINESS DOES NOT DIFFER
FROM FORM AND FORM DOES
NOT DIFFER FROM EMPTINESS.
WHATEVER IS FORM, THAT IS
EMPTINESS AND WHATEVER IS
EMPTINESS, THAT IS FORM.
                    —Avalokiteshvara

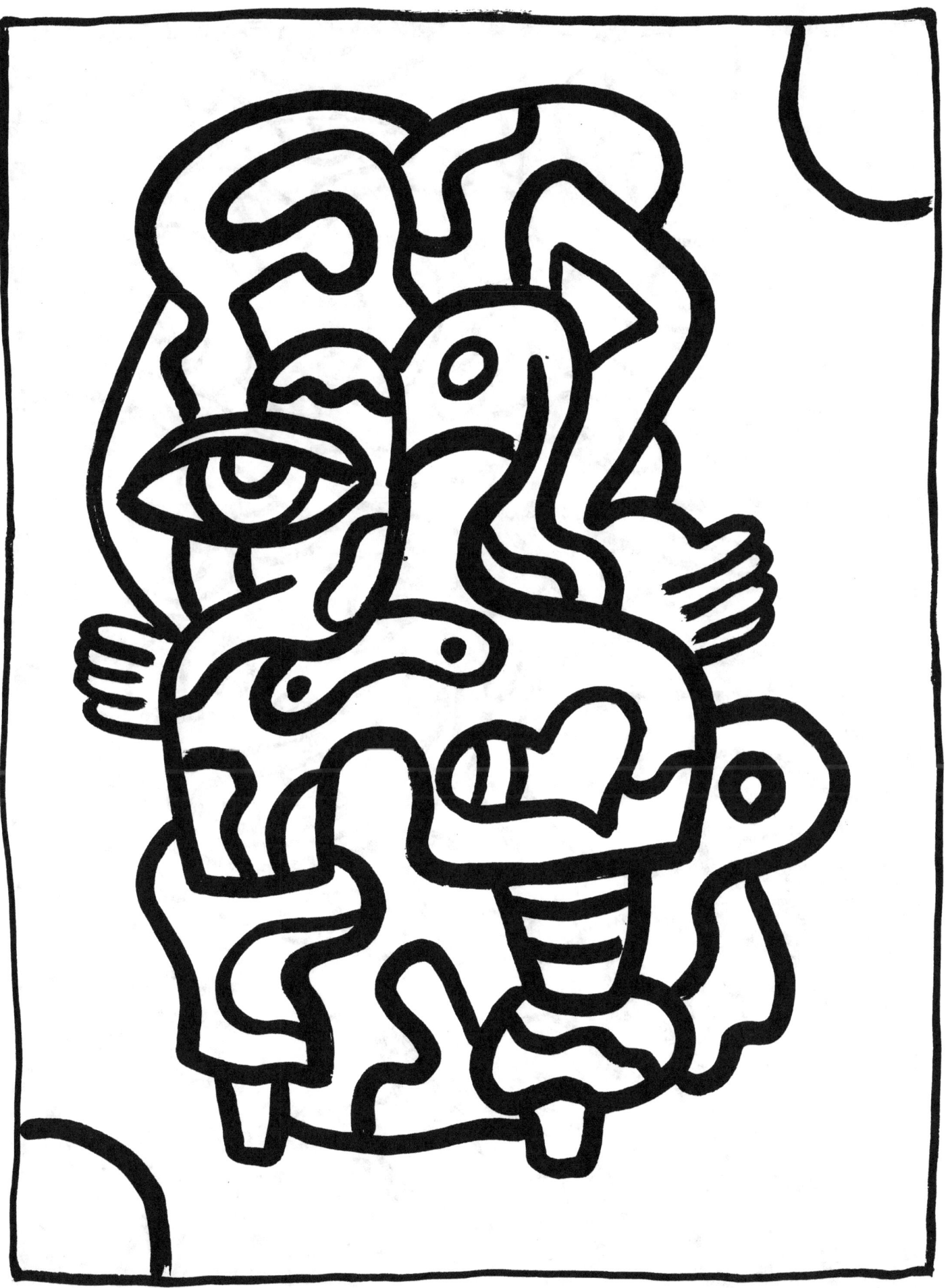

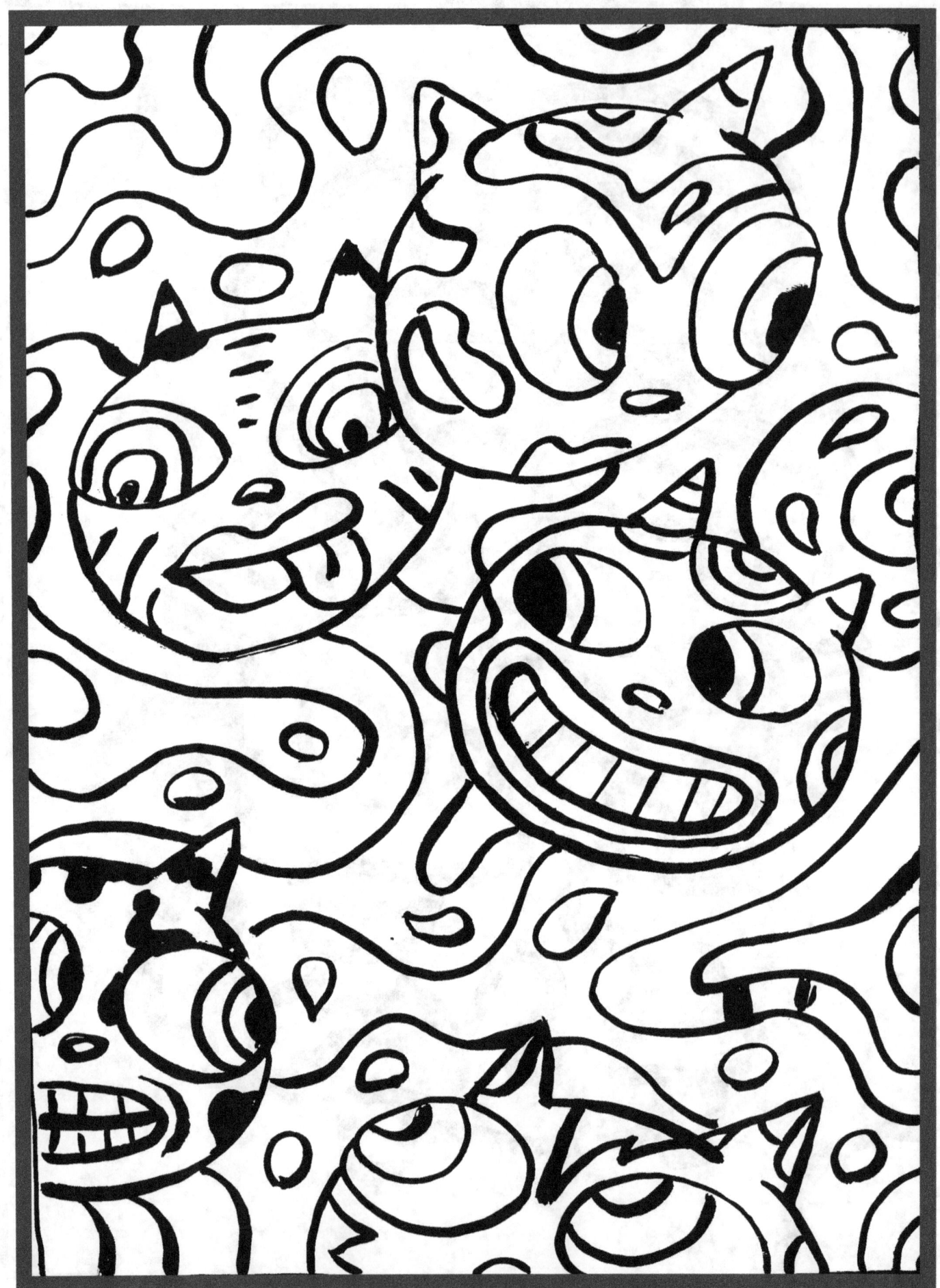

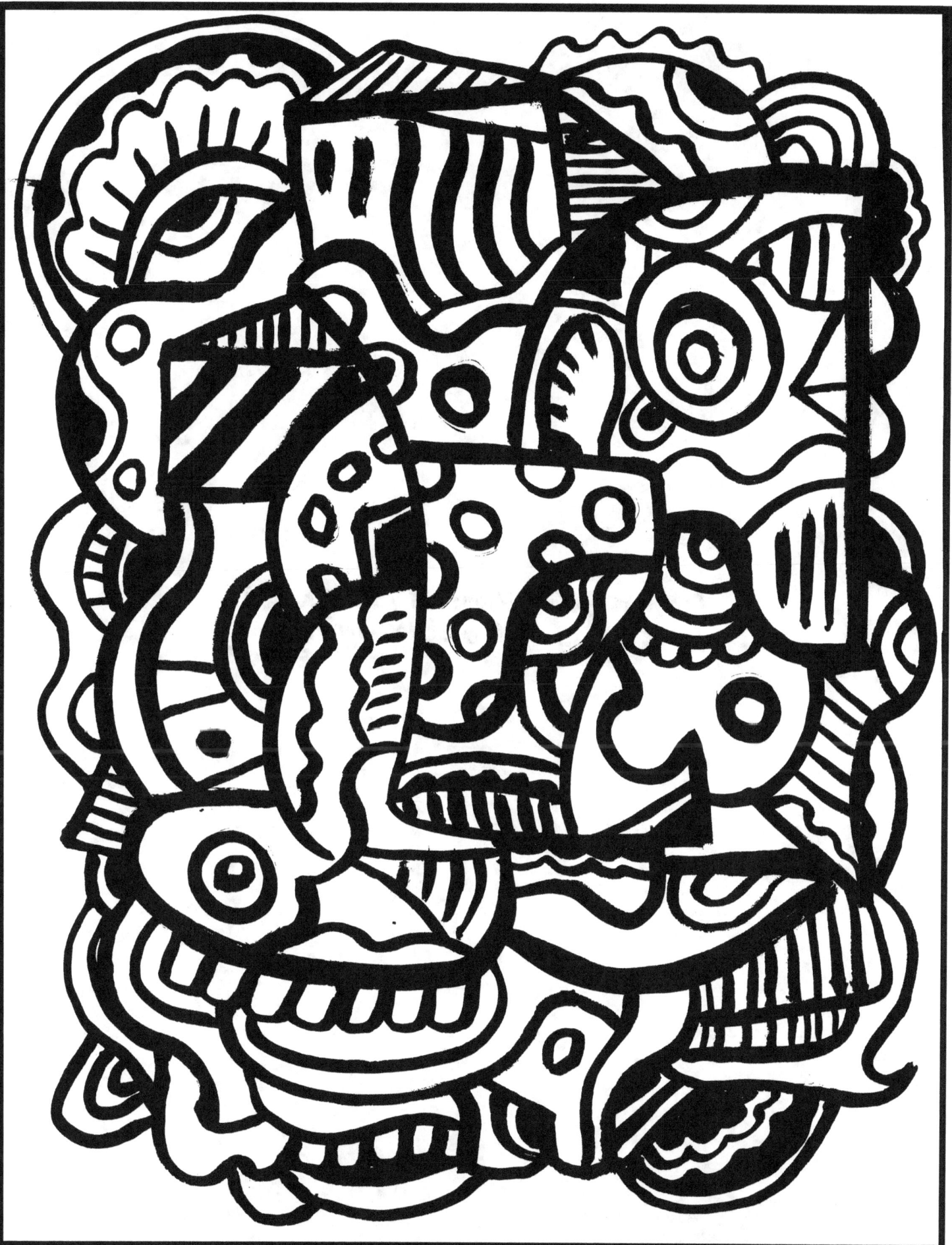

IN MY BEGINNING IS MY END. IN
MY END IS MY BEGINNING.
                          —T.S. ELLIOT

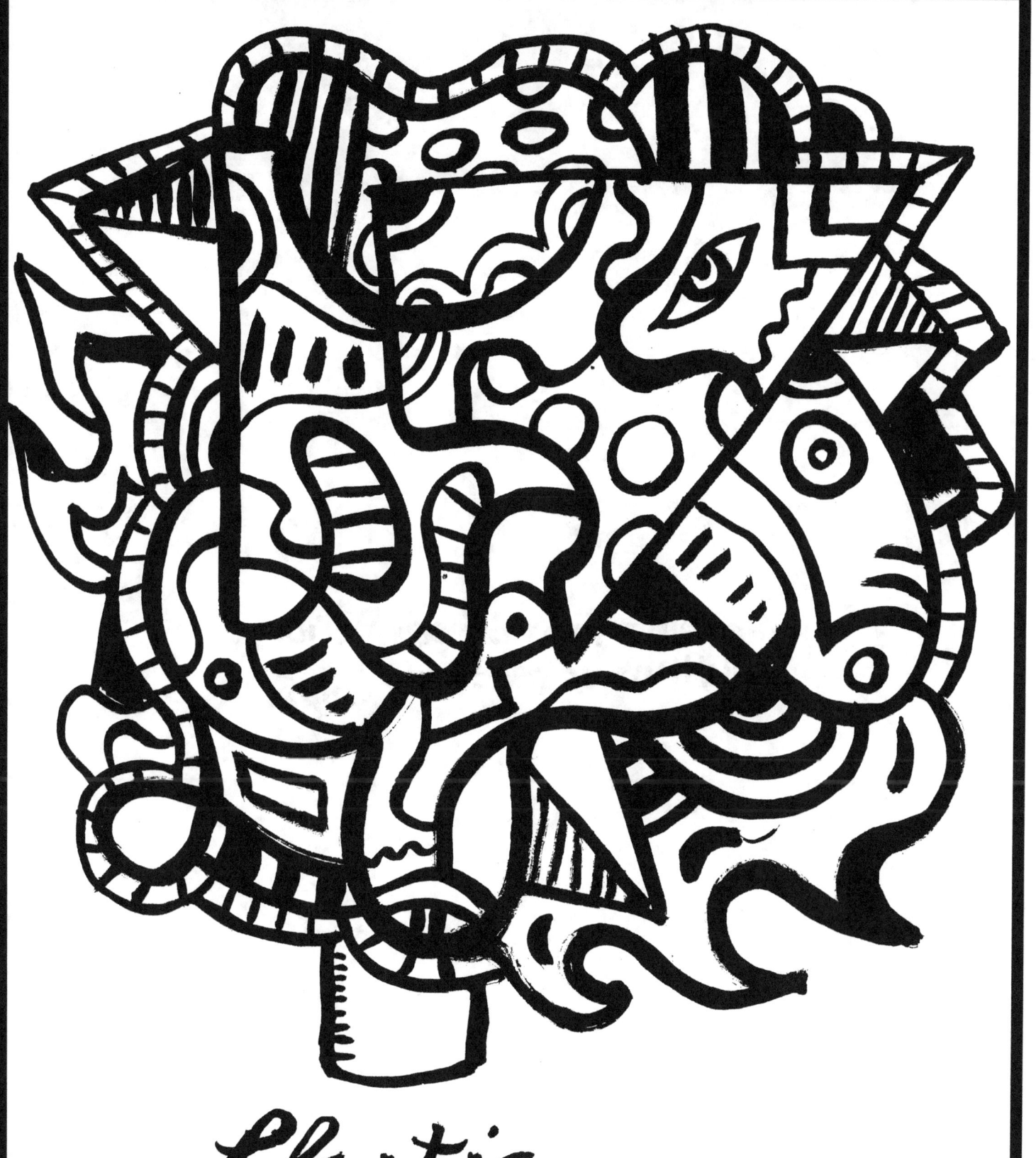

plastic
manifestations

Have no fear of perfection,
you'll never reach it. —DALI

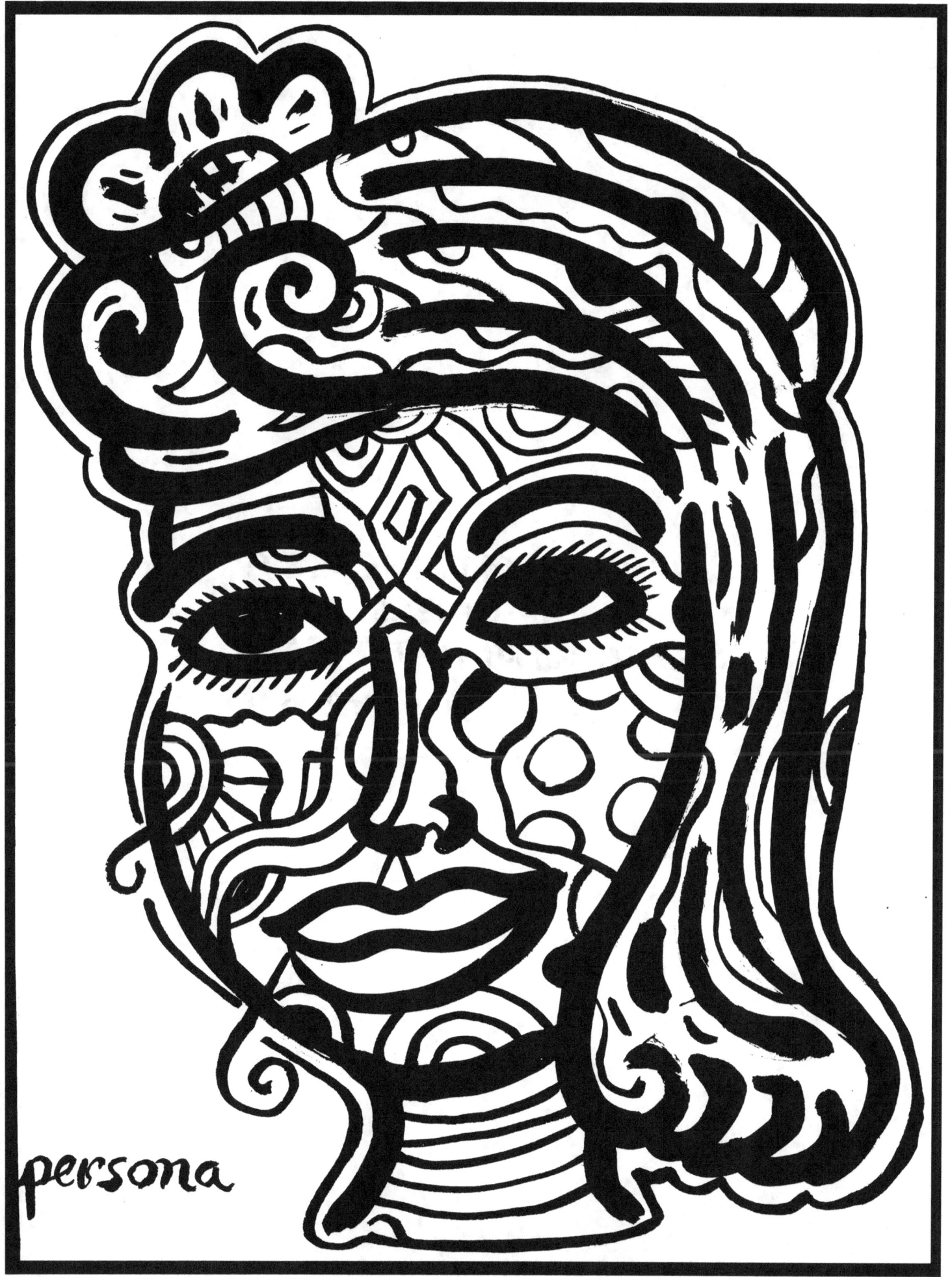

persona

WHEN I PAINT, THE SEA
ROARS. THE OTHERS JUST
SPLASH ABOUT IN THE BATH.

-SALVADOR DALI

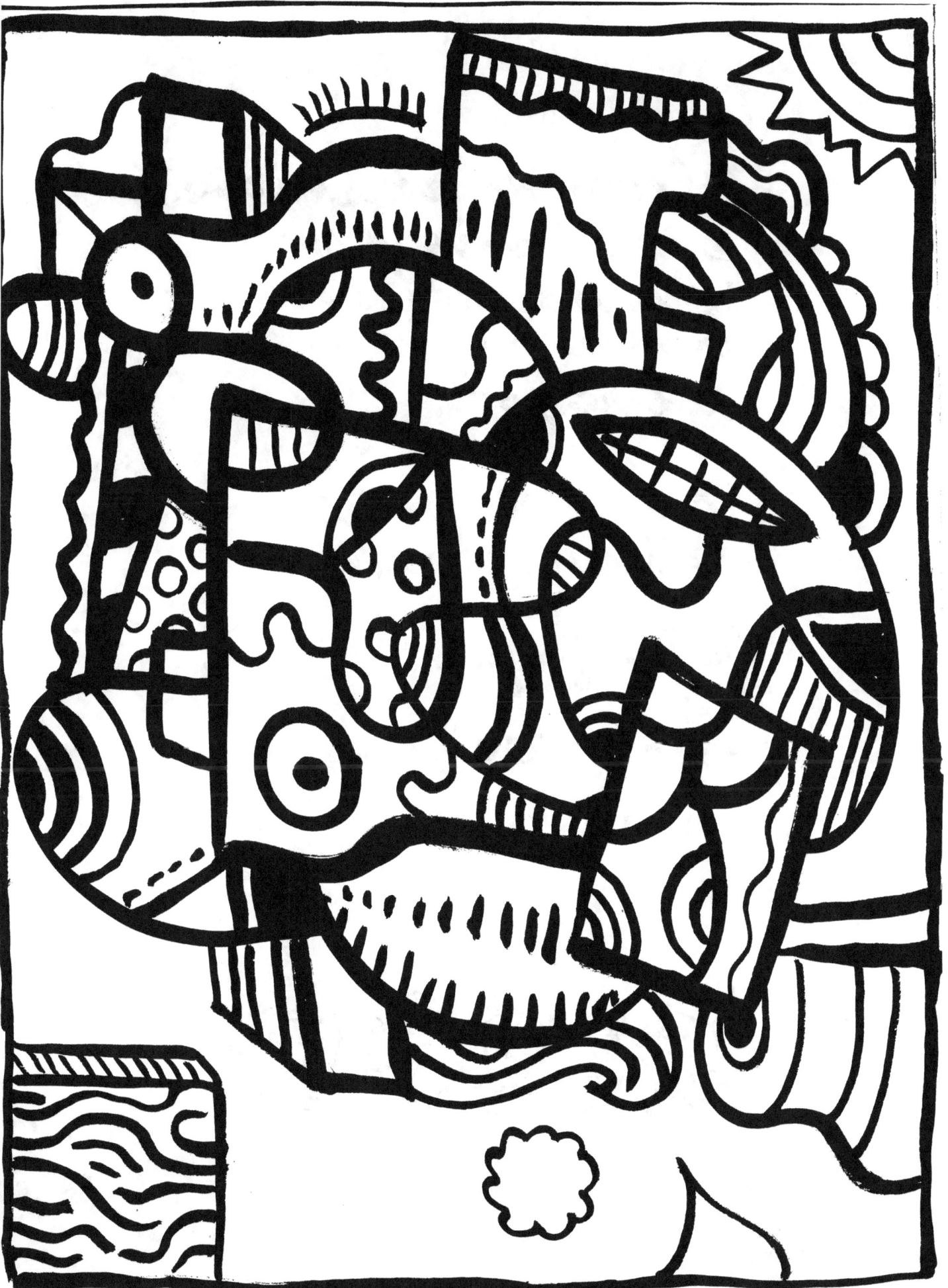

Leonardo takes the cake.
Is it not so very so.
Leonardo takes the cake.
Oh where oh where
did he go?

A bird in flight
and dreams so real.

As he flays

in the dead

of night.

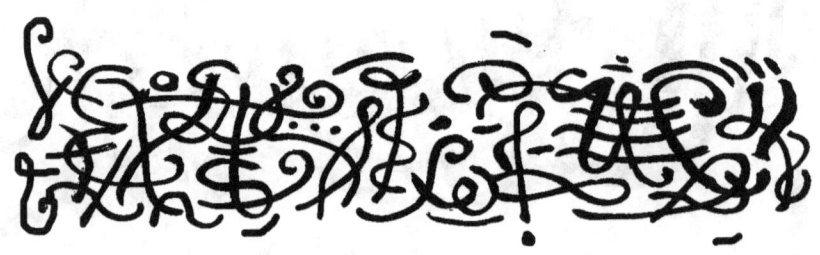

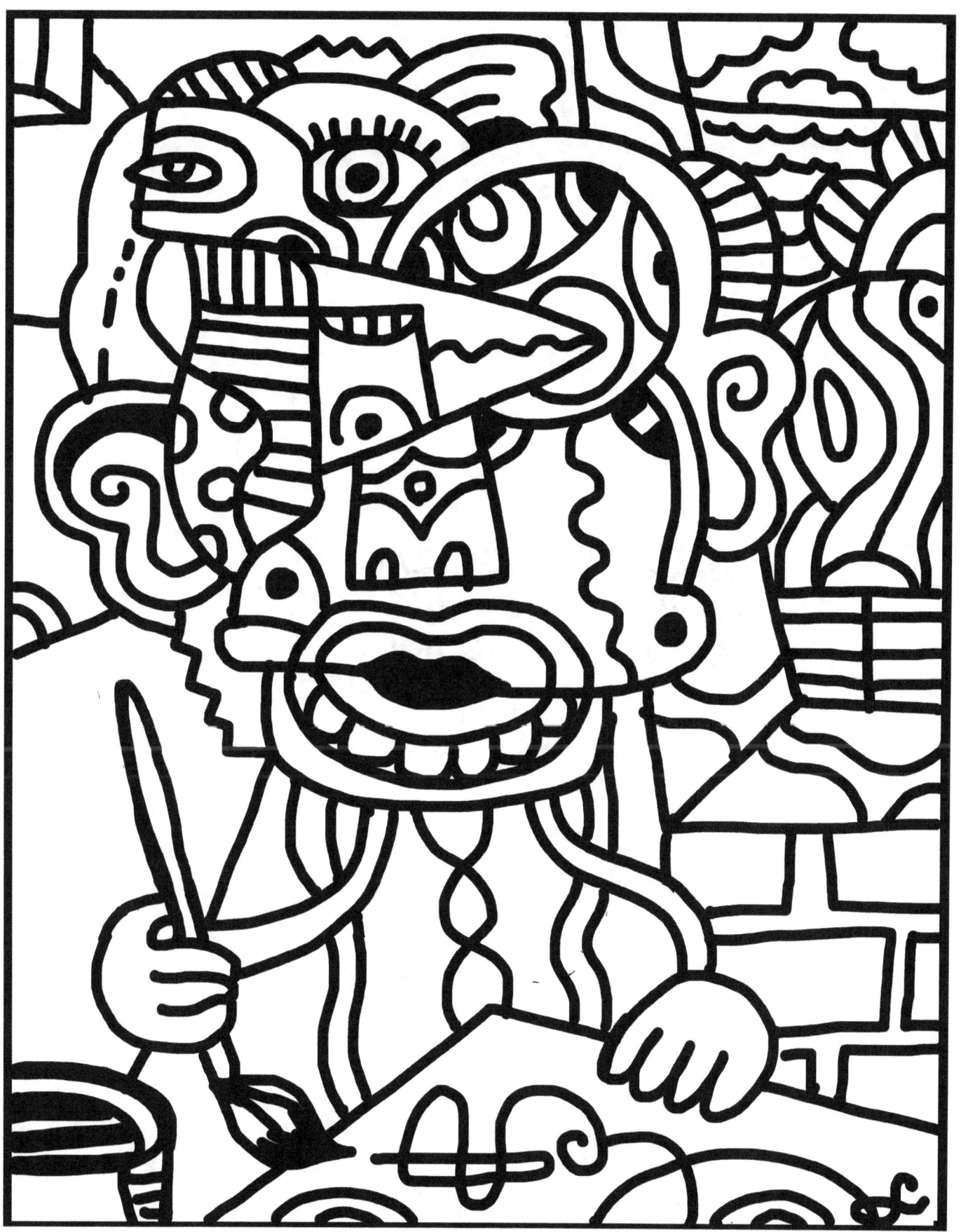

THREE THINGS CANNOT BE
LONG HIDDEN: THE SUN, THE
MOON AND THE TRUTH.
                    —BUDDHISM

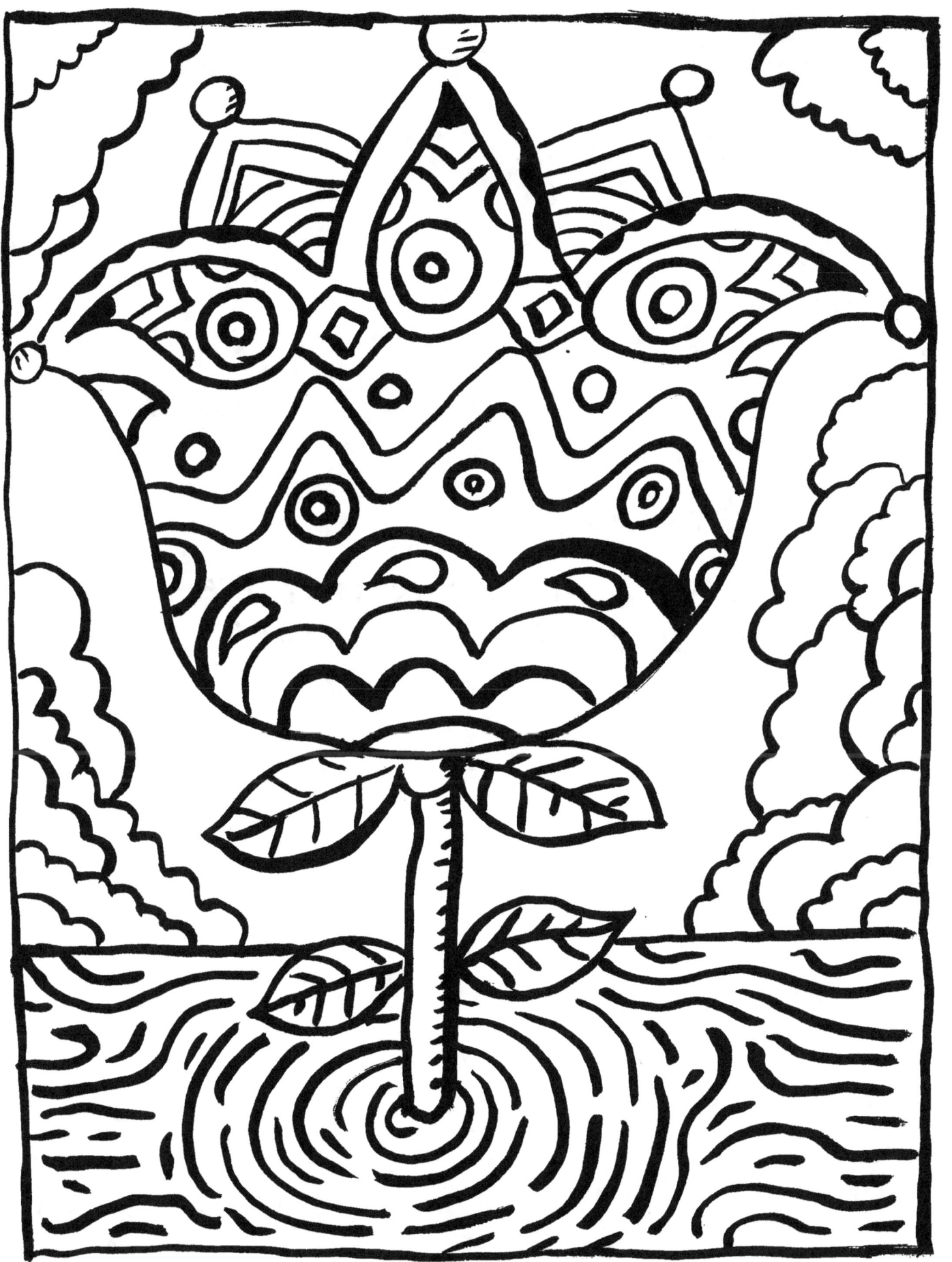

TO THE MIND THAT IS STILL, THE
WHOLE UNIVERSE SURRENDERS.

– LAO TZU

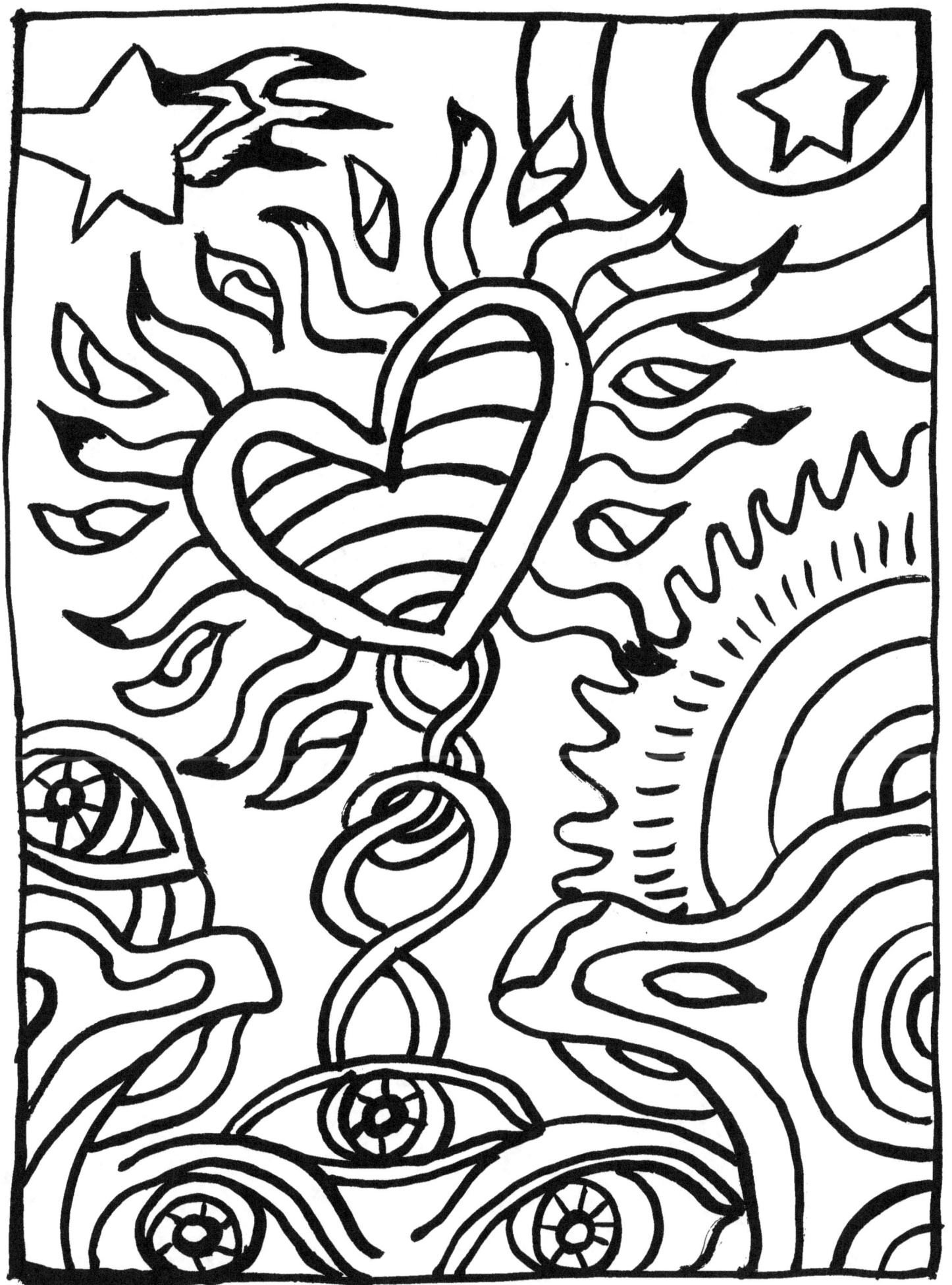

At the still point,
there the dance is.

— T.S. Elliott

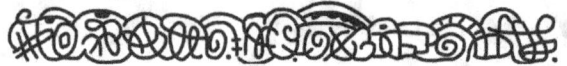

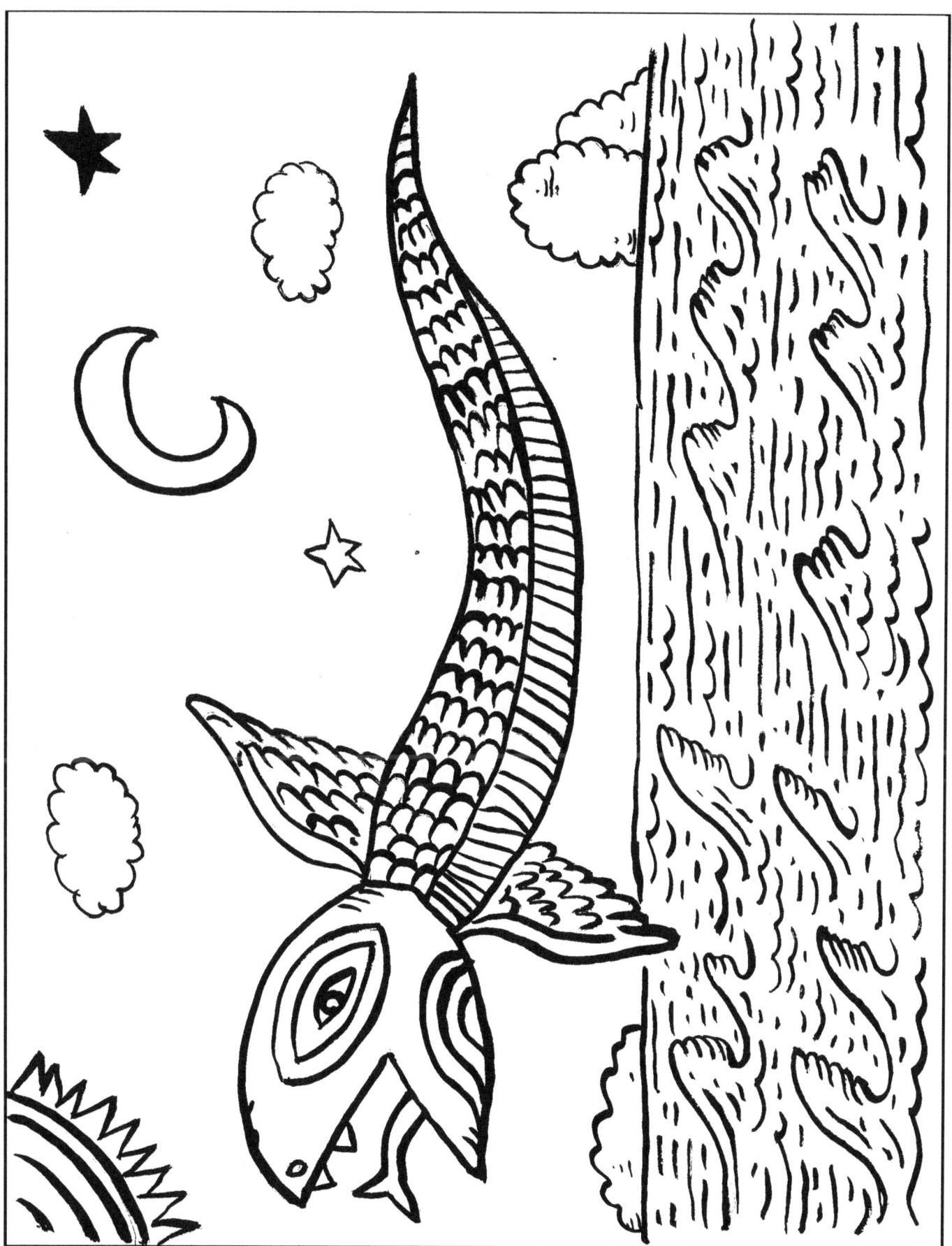

Do I Believe in God?
Yes, when I Paint.

—Henri
Matisse

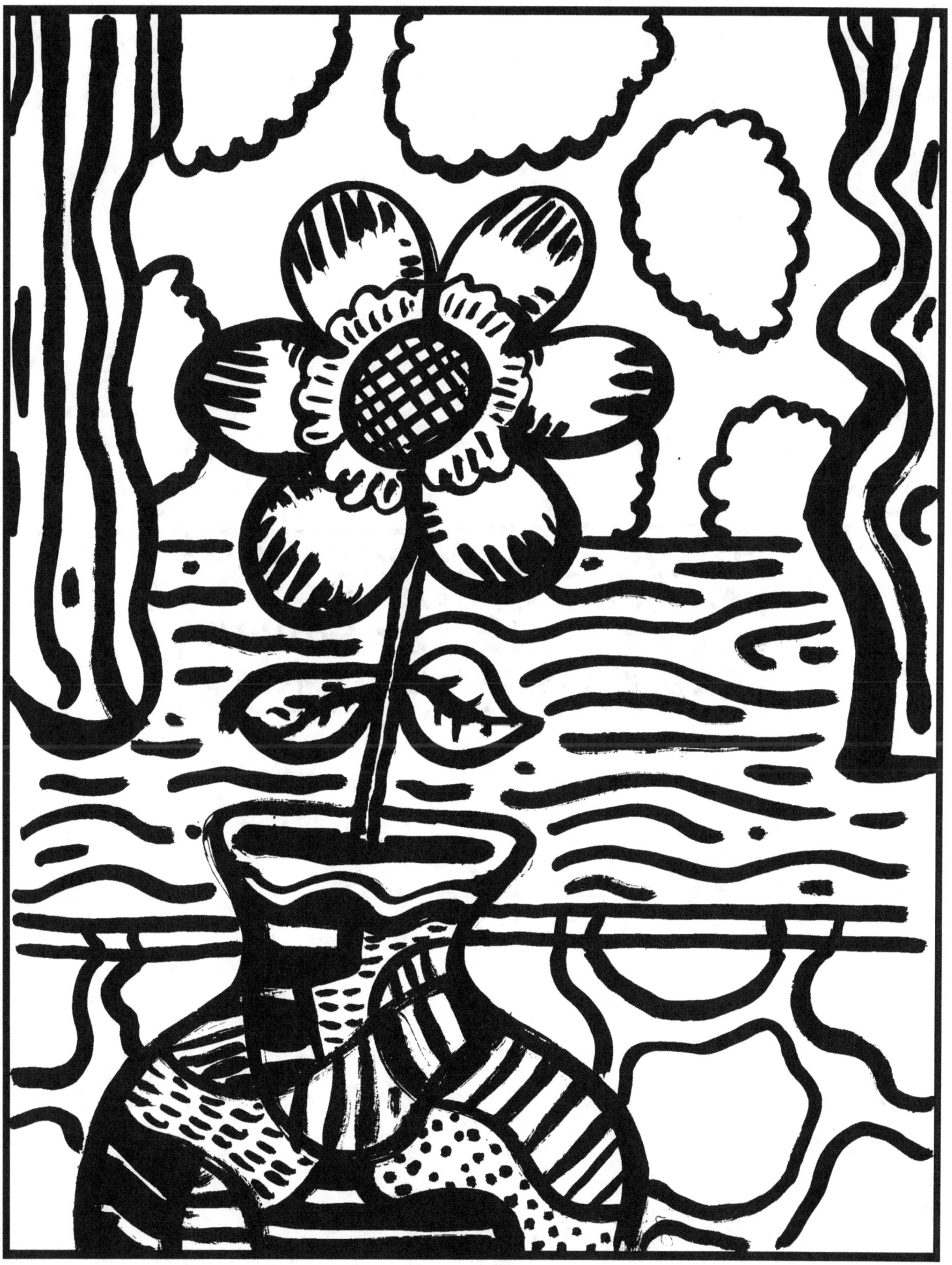

THERE IS ONLY ONE WAY
TO AVOID CRITICISM:
DO NOTHING, SAY NOTHING
AND BE NOTHING. - ARISTOTLE

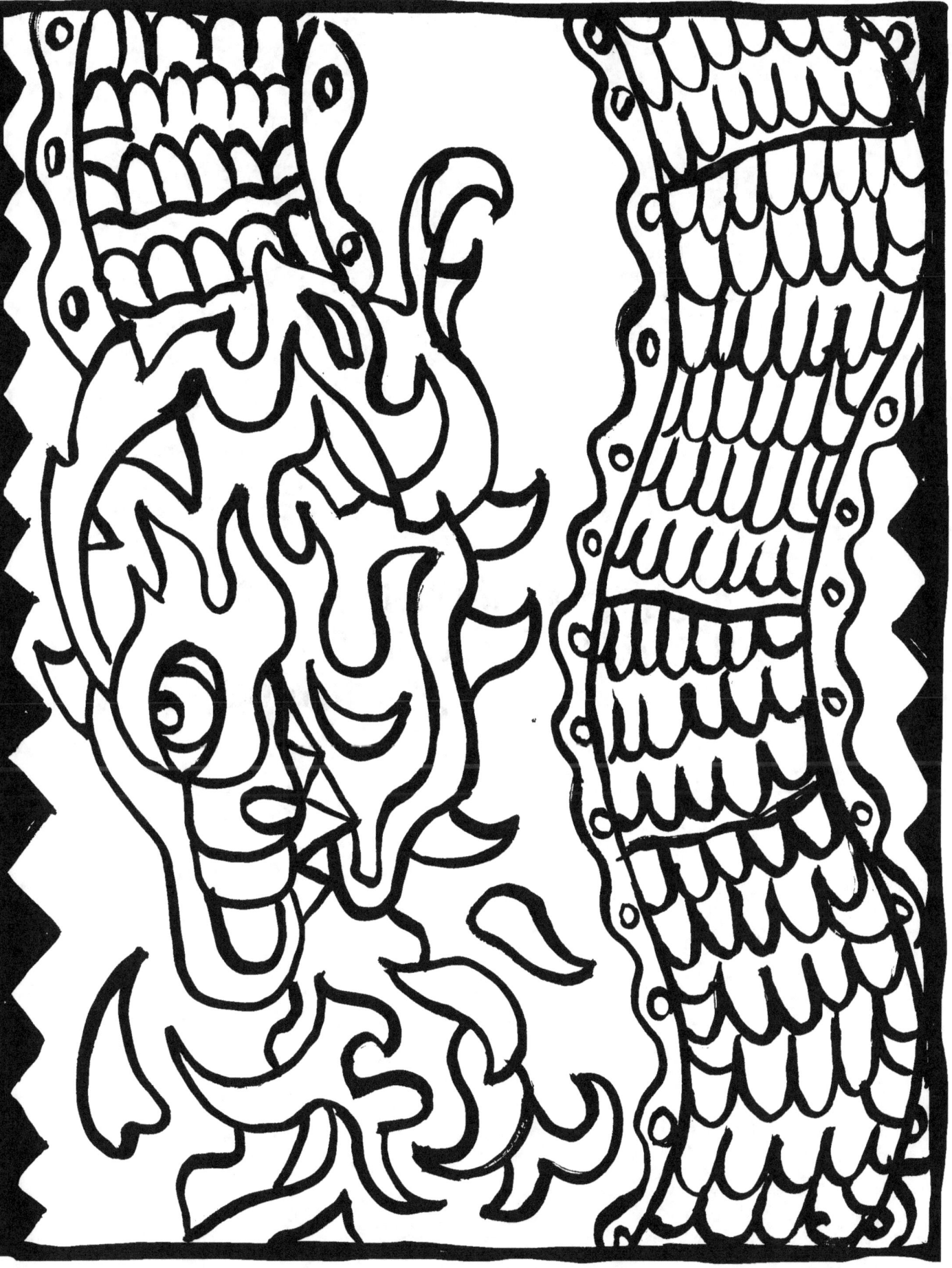

A STRONG IMAGINATION
BEGETS THE EVENT.
— Montaigne

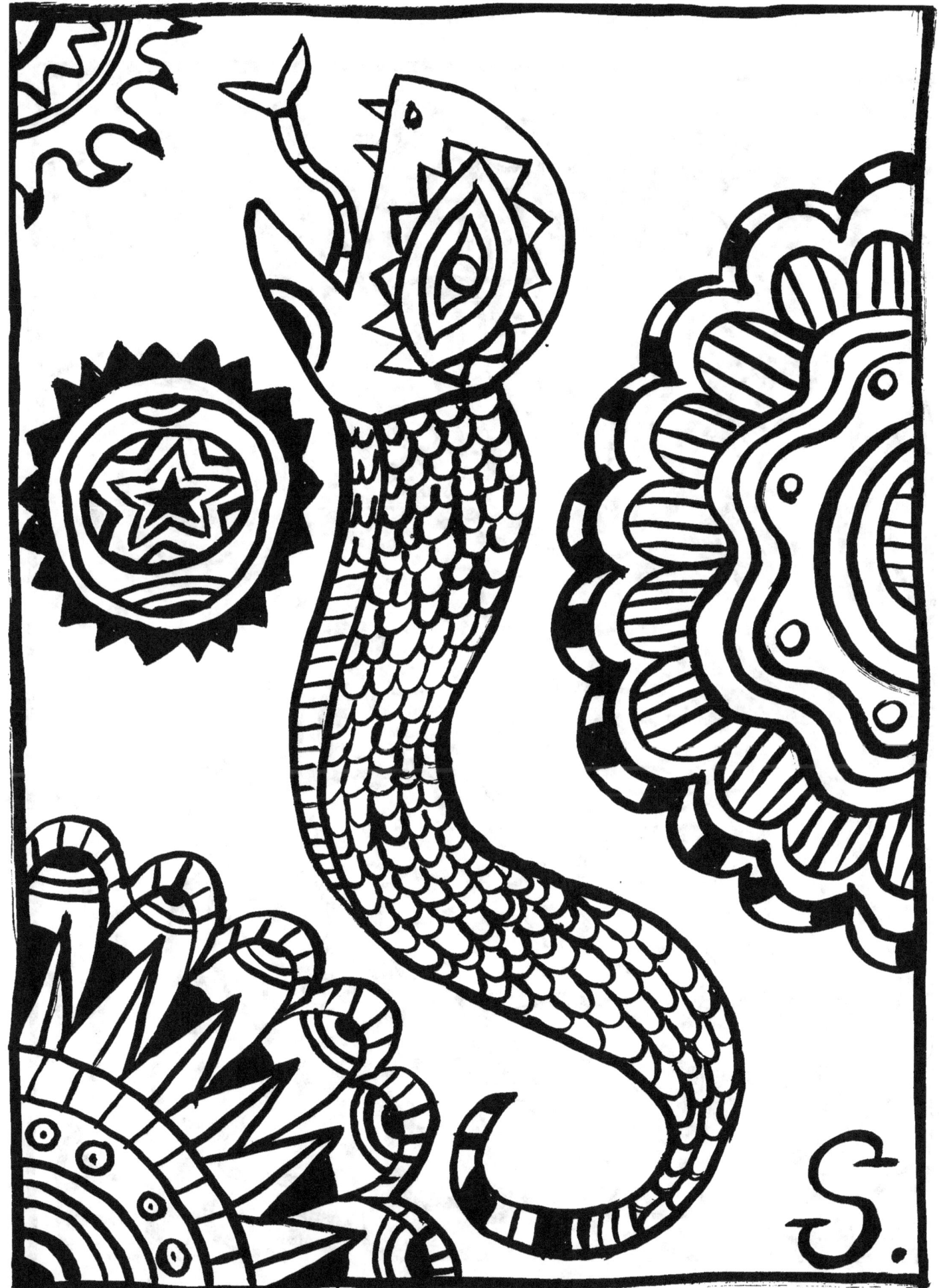

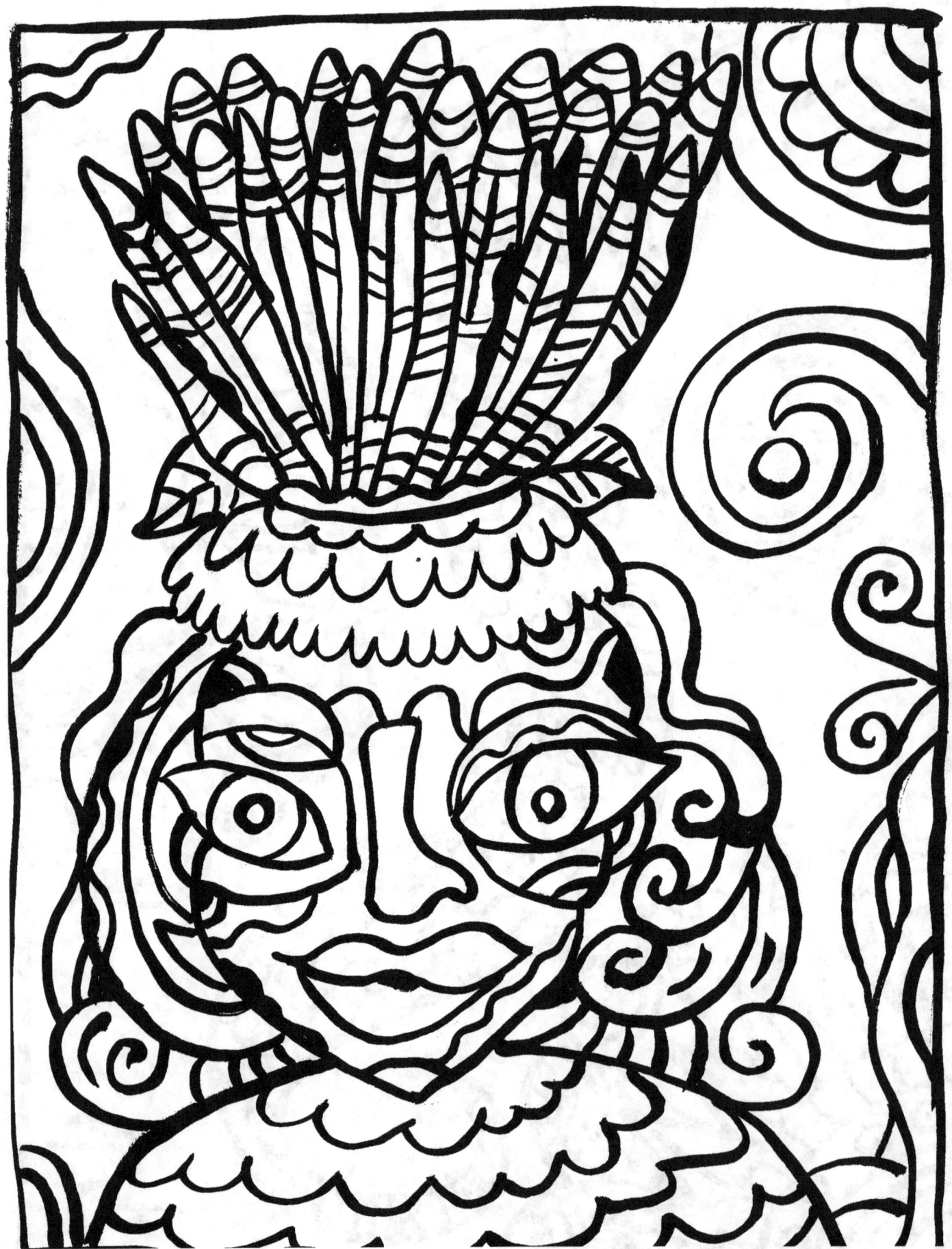

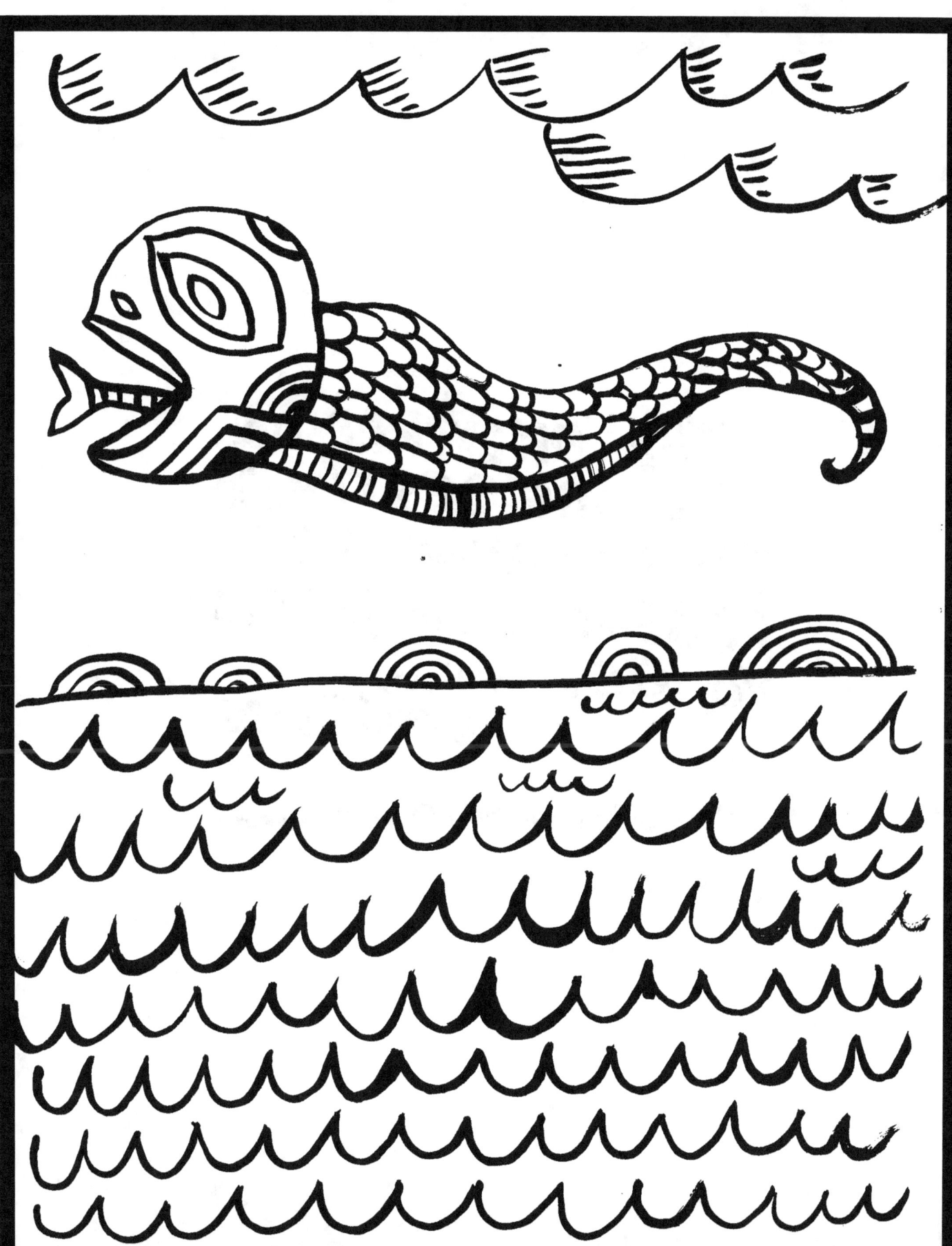

THE ONLY PERSON
YOU ARE DESTINED
TO BECOME IS THE
PERSON YOU DECIDE
TO BE. — R.W.
           EMERSON

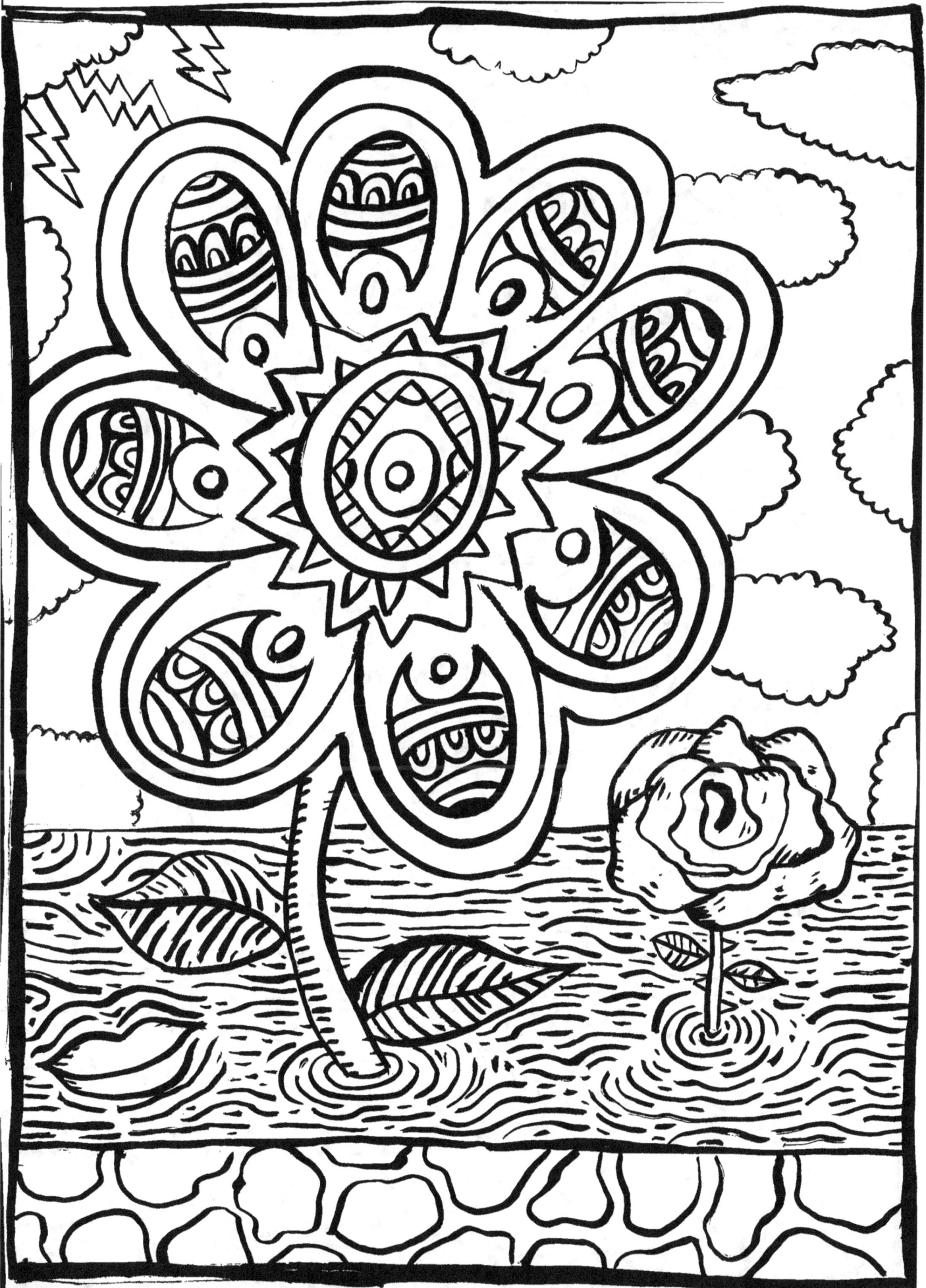

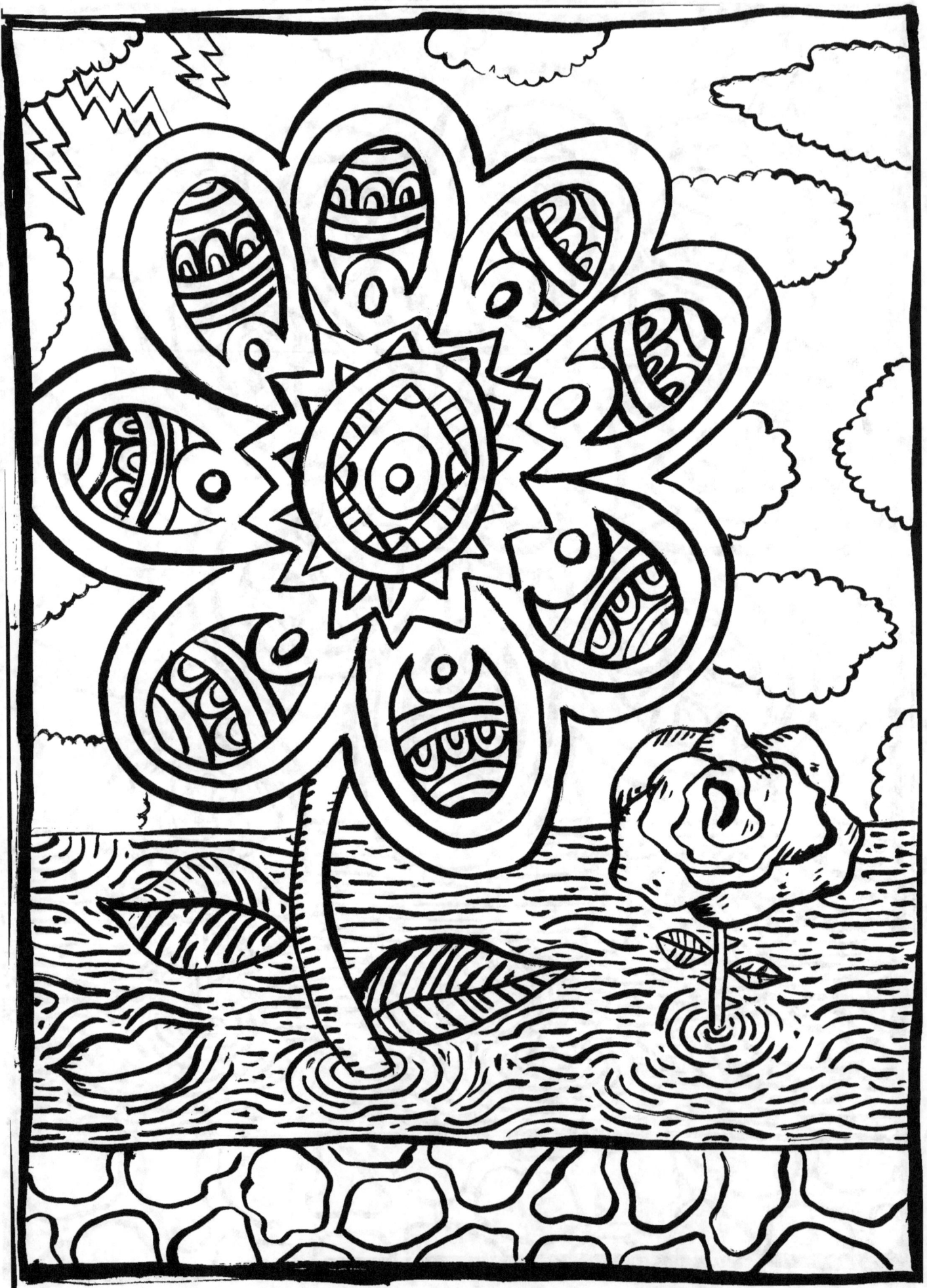

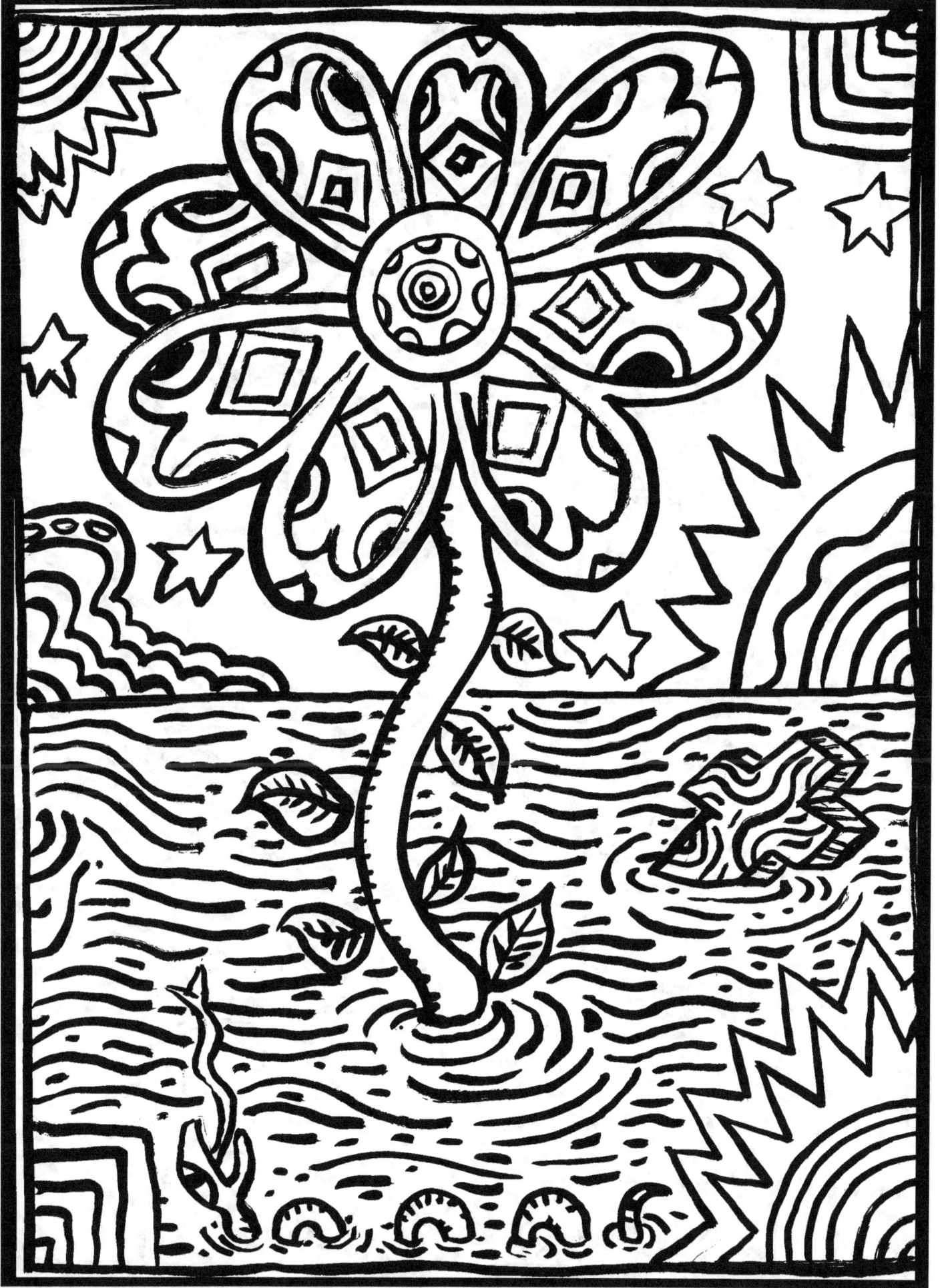

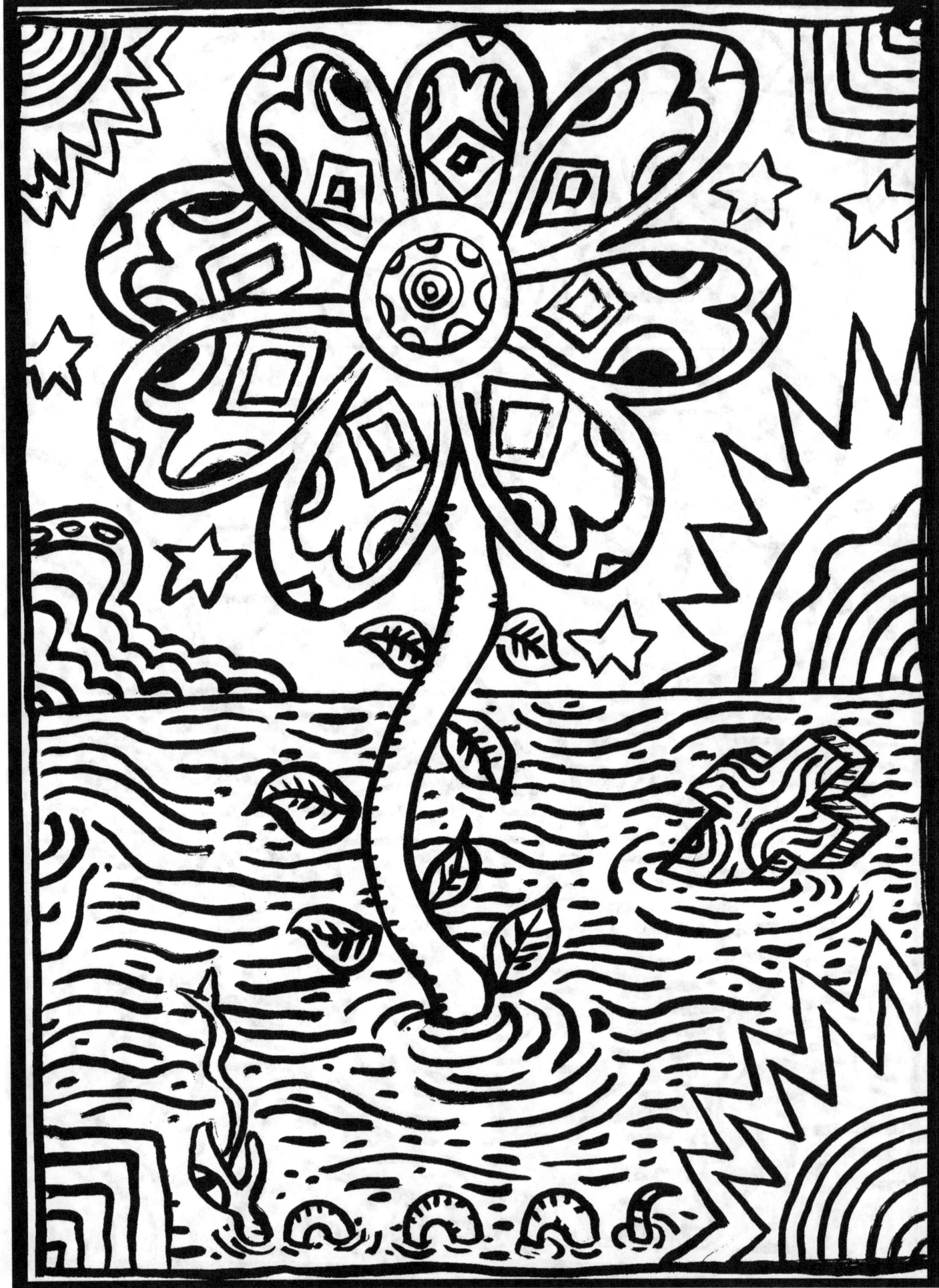

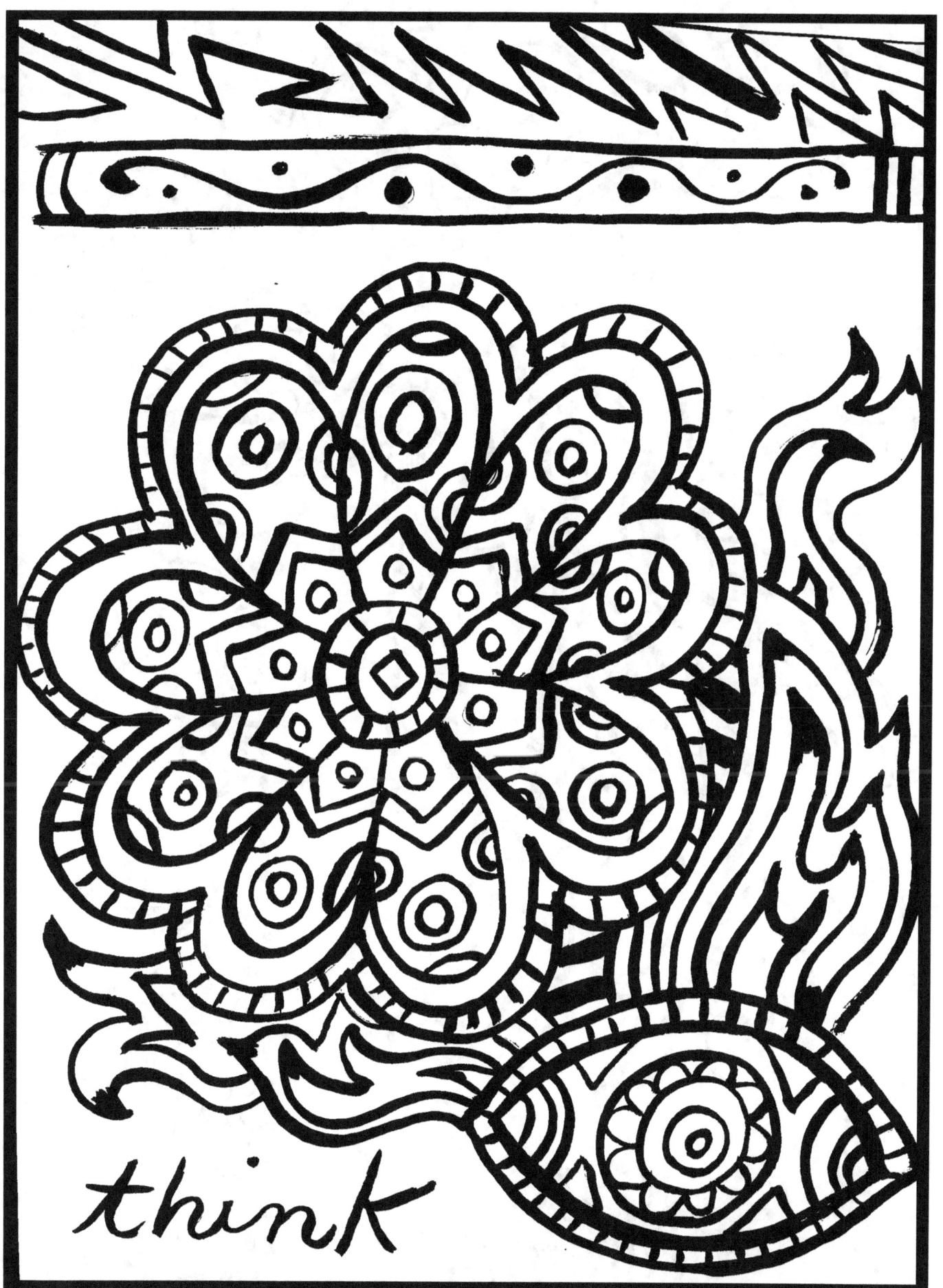

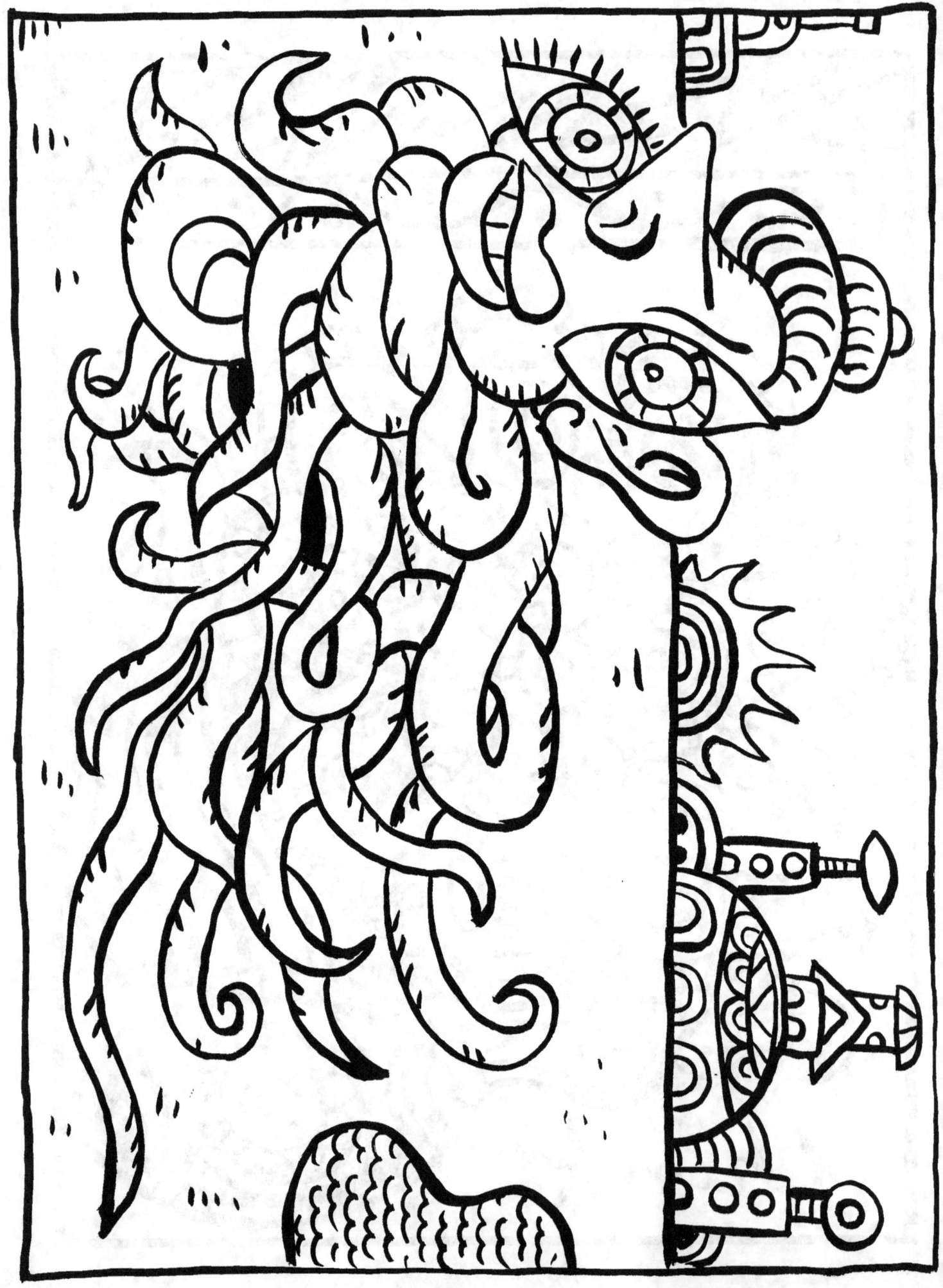

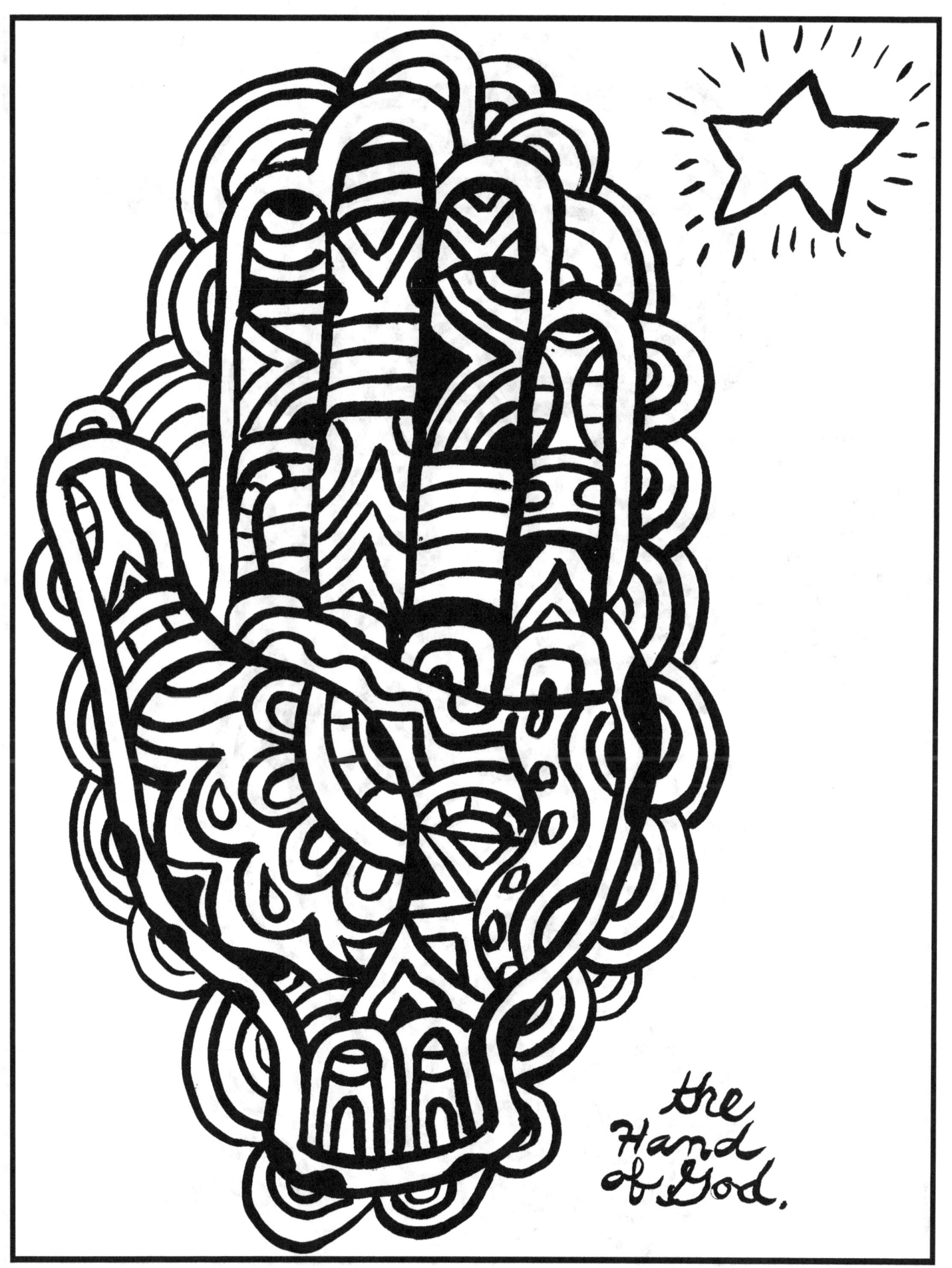

the
Hand
of God.

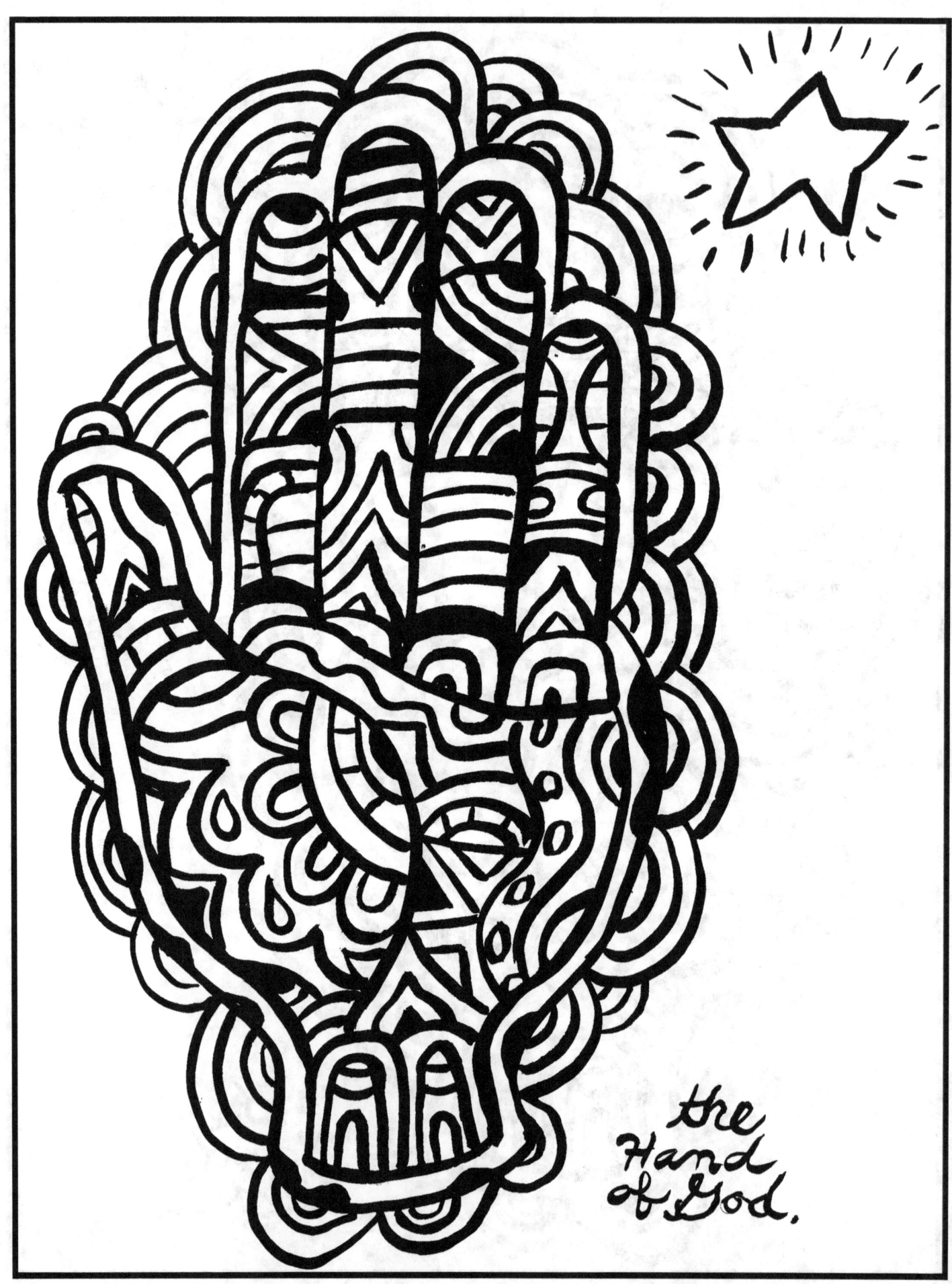

the
Hand
of God.

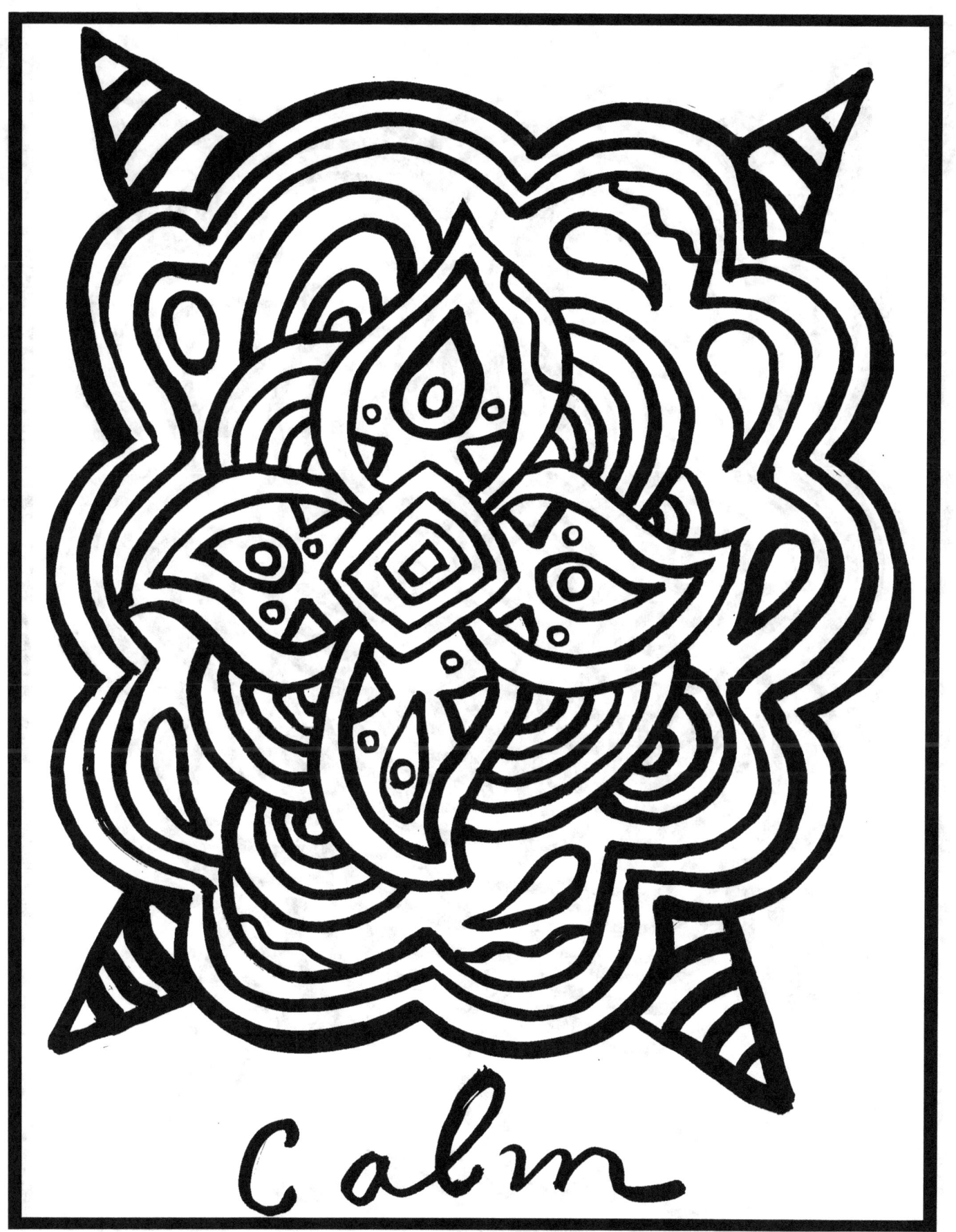

Calm

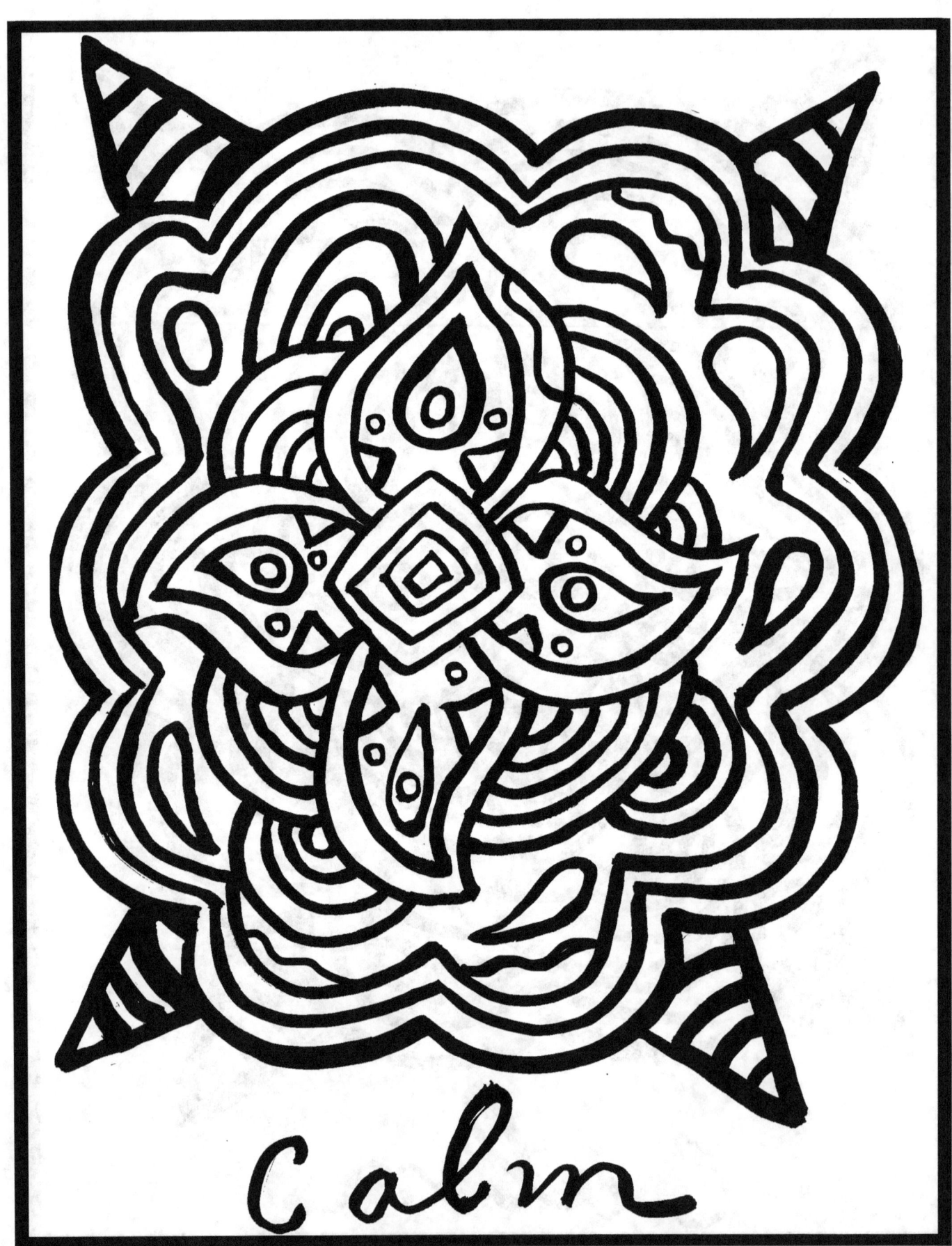

Calm

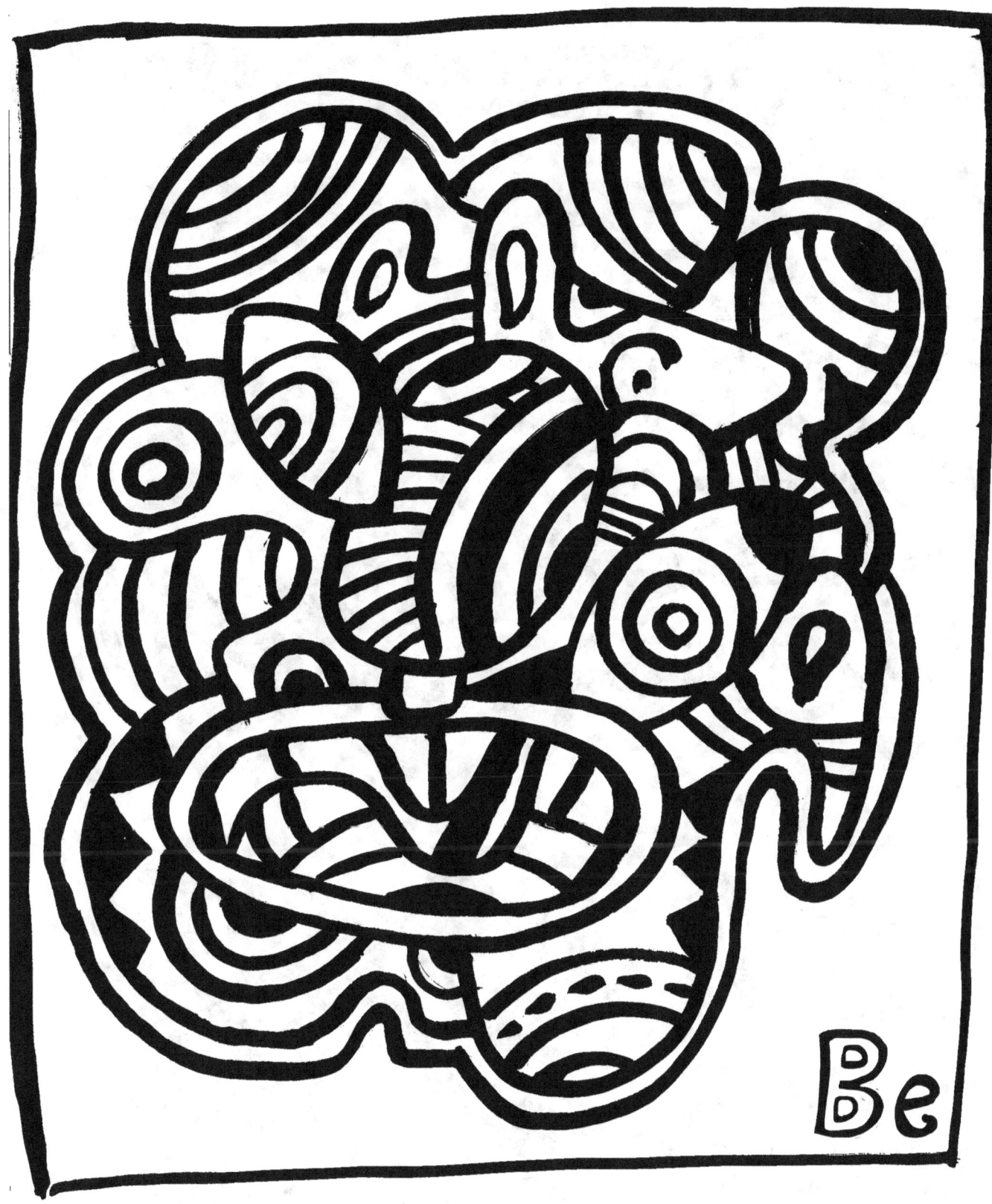

Art is not reality

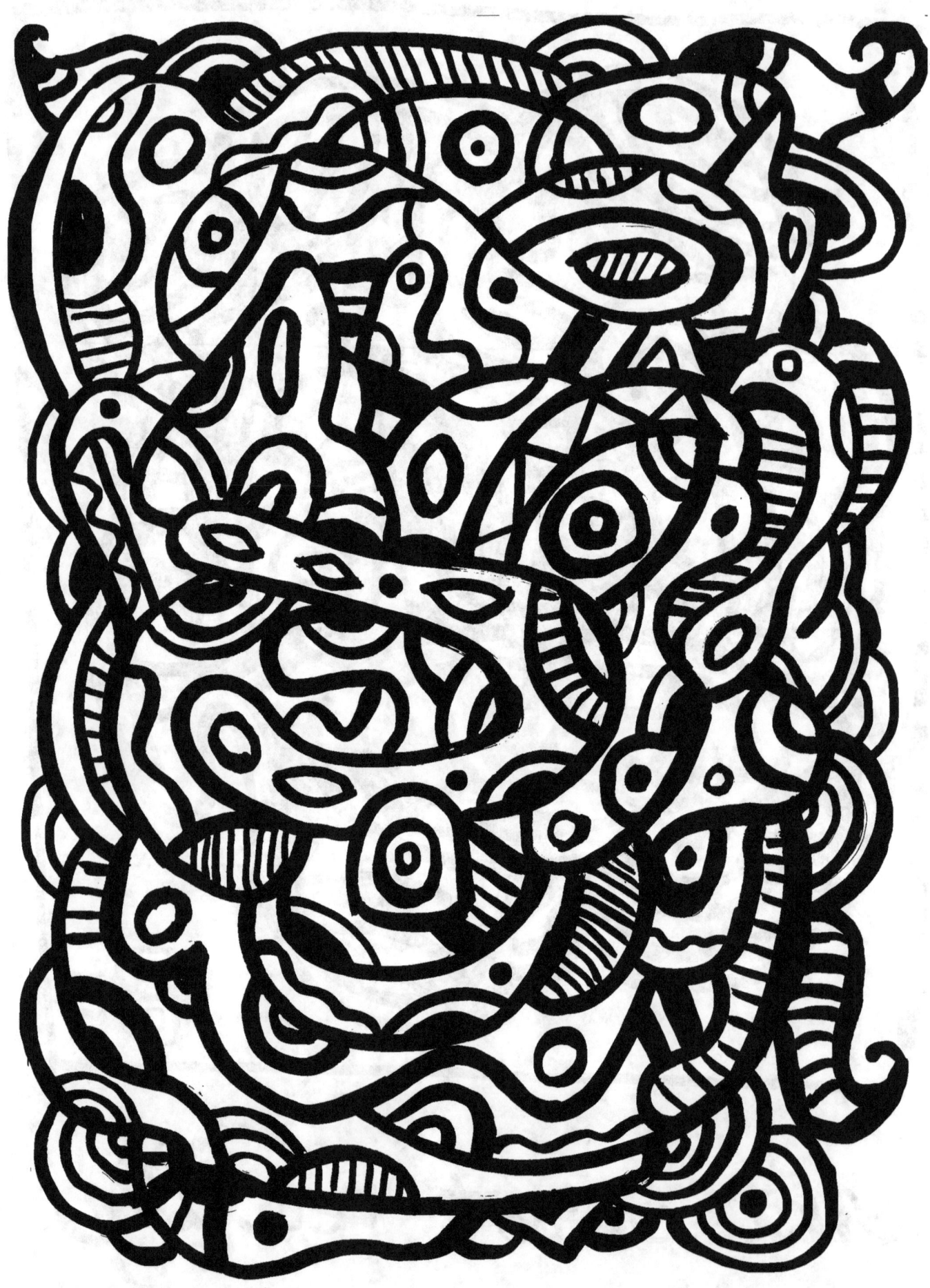

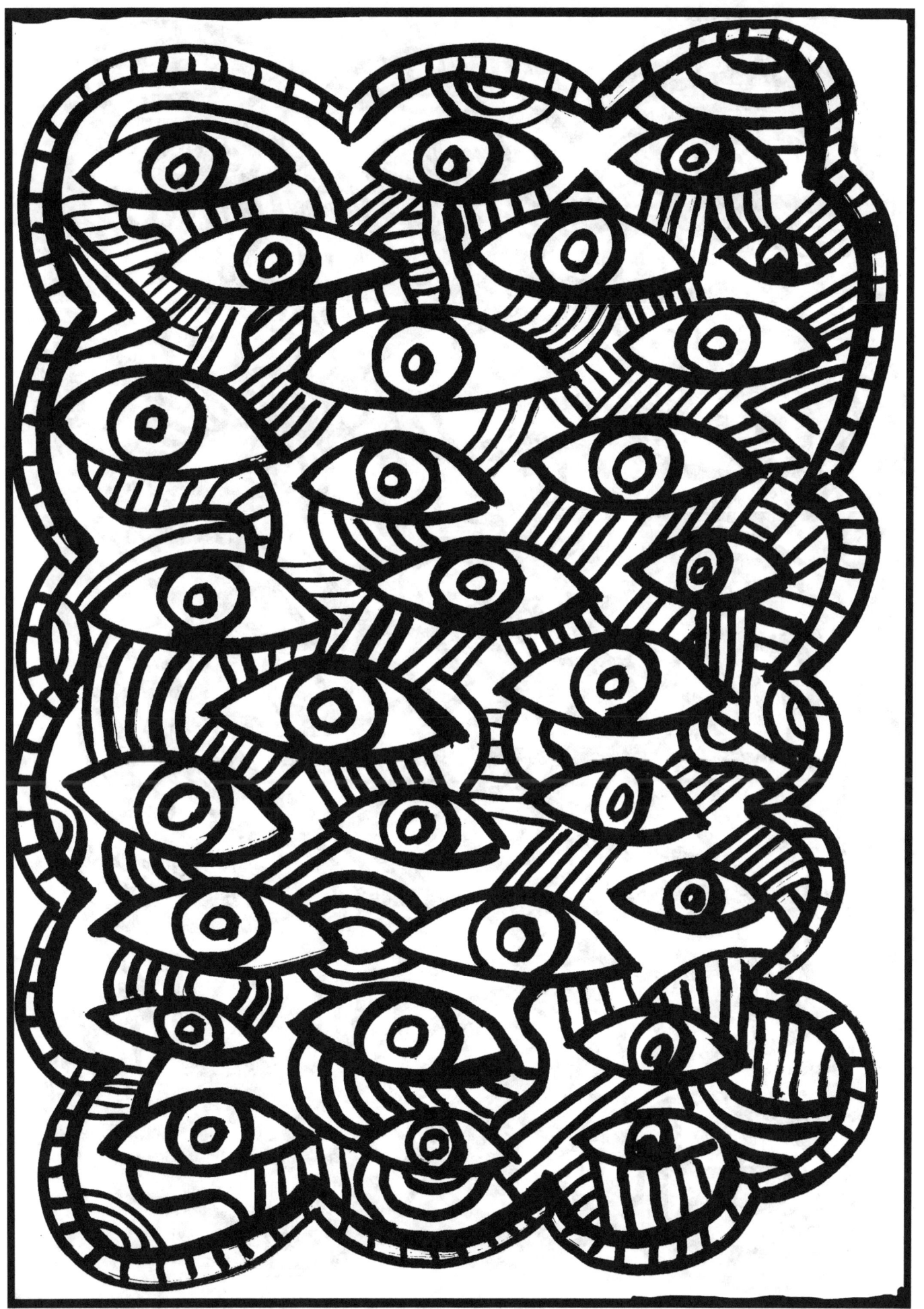

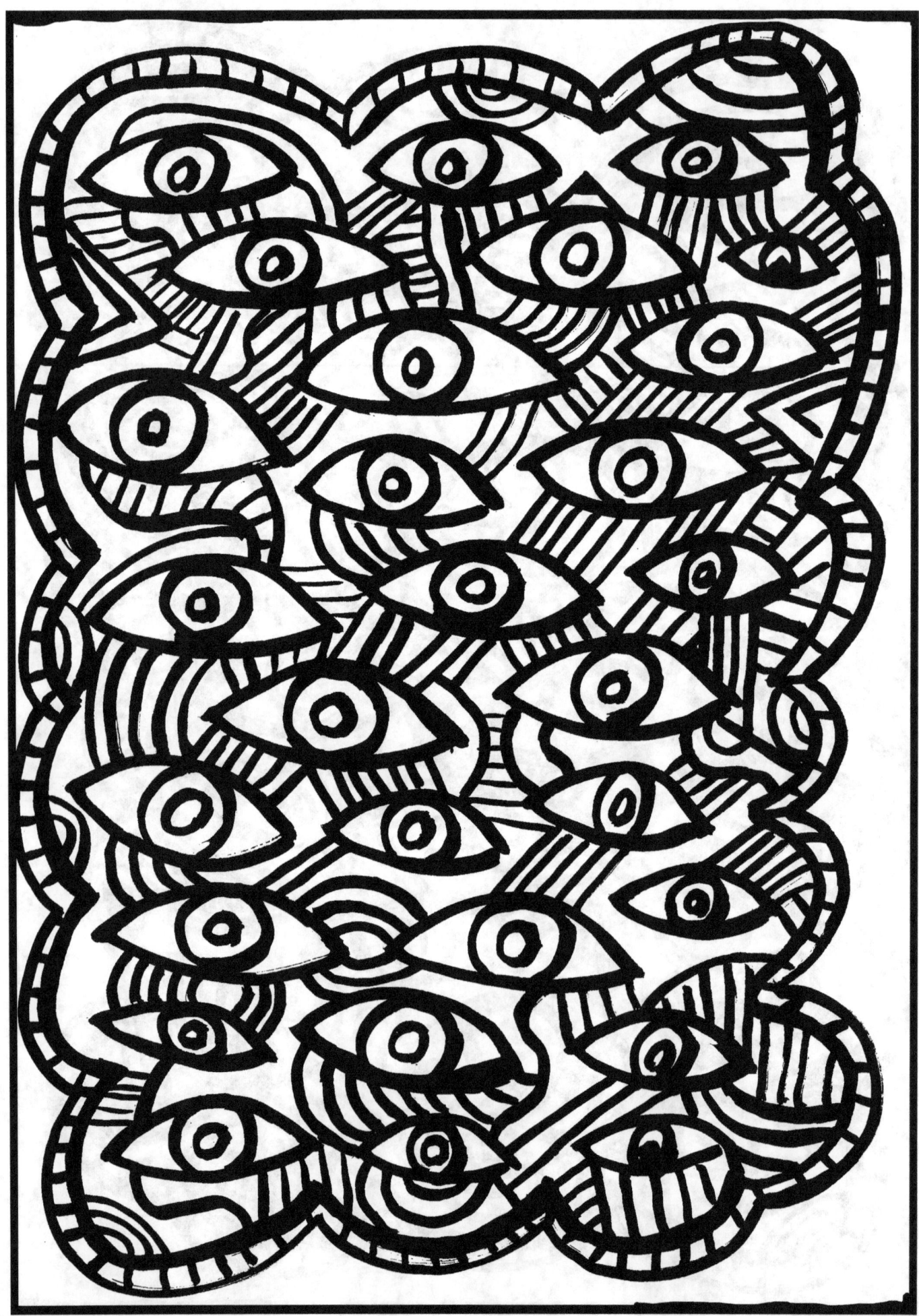

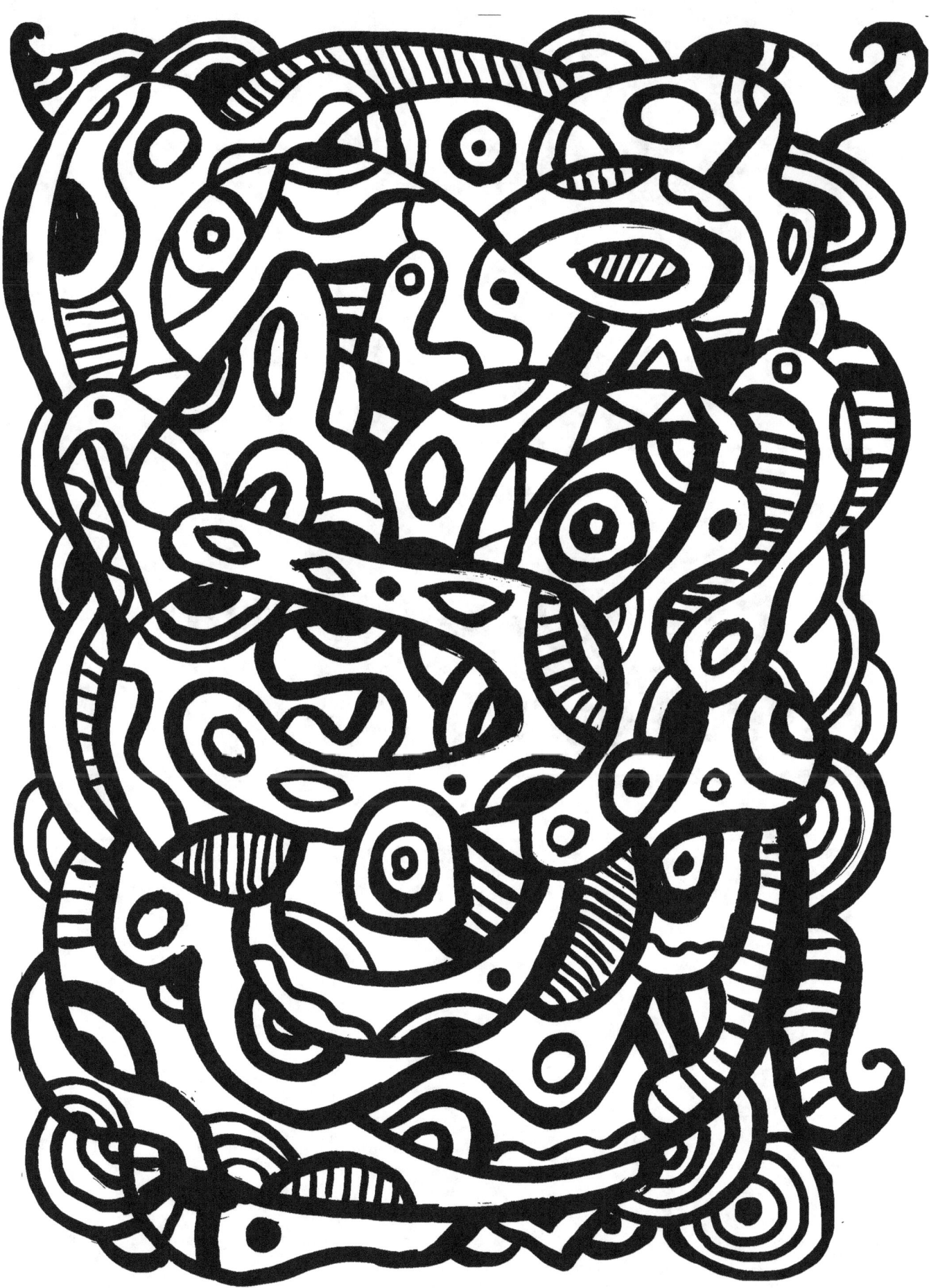

Energy is eternal delight. —BLAKE

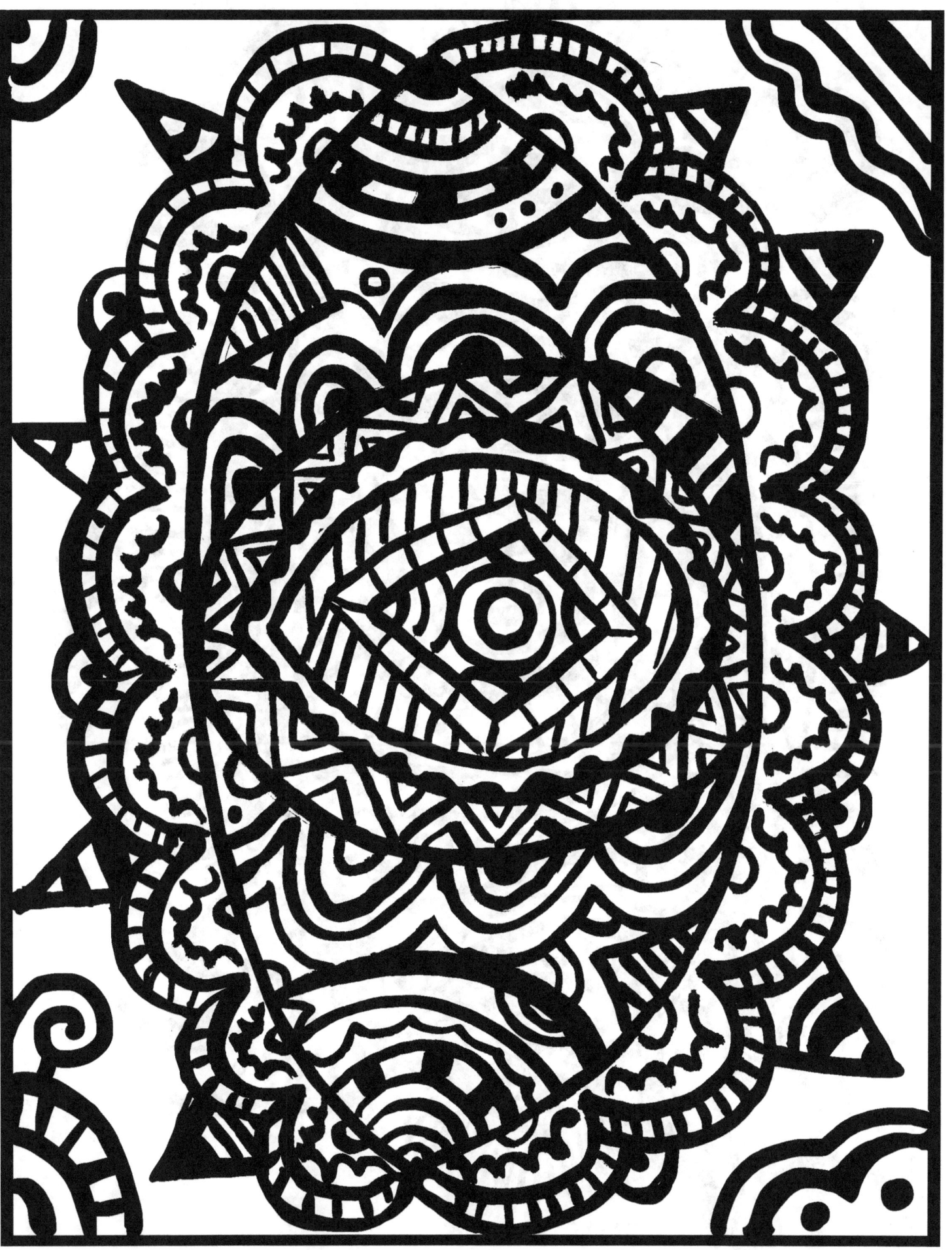

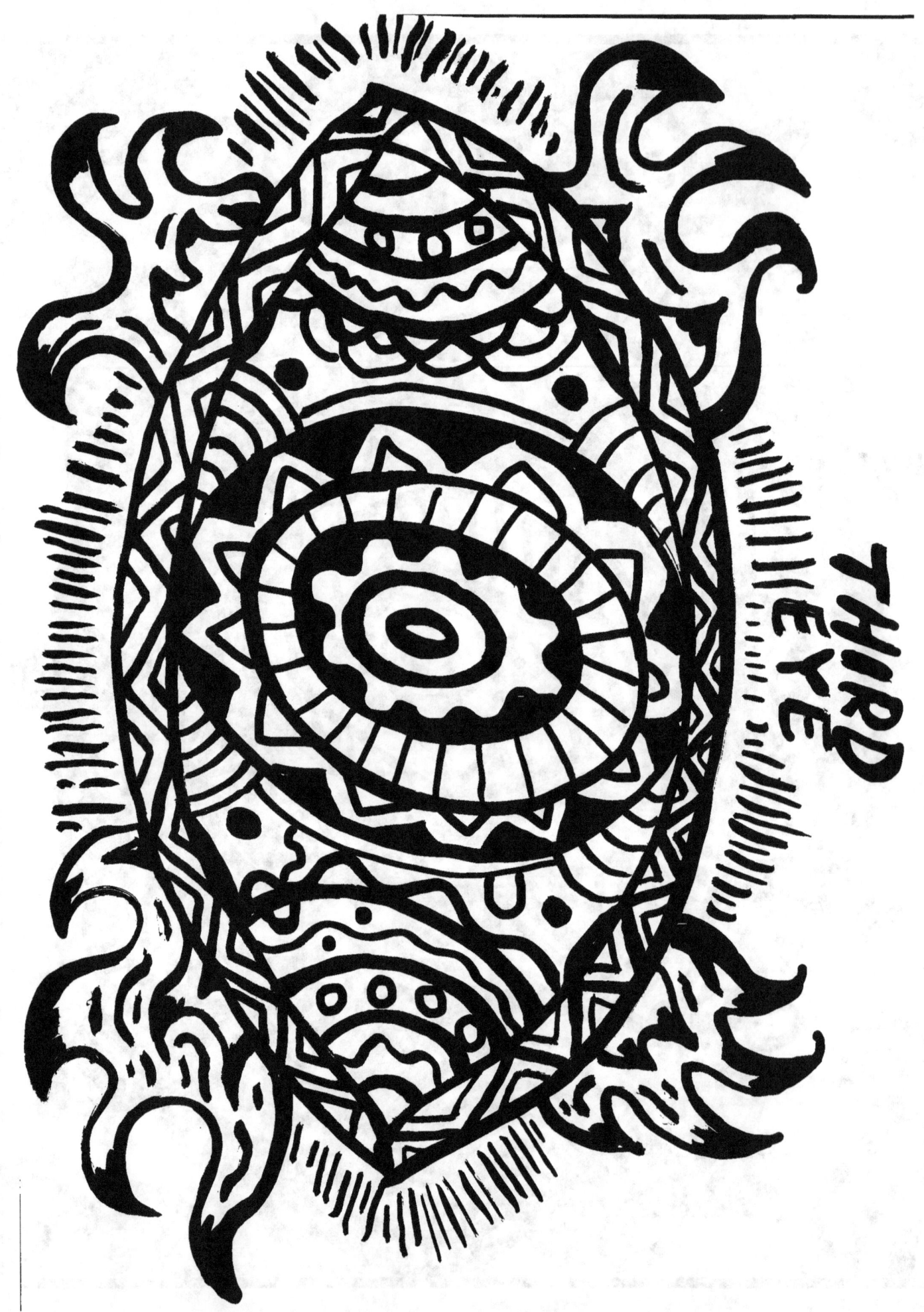

THIRD EYE

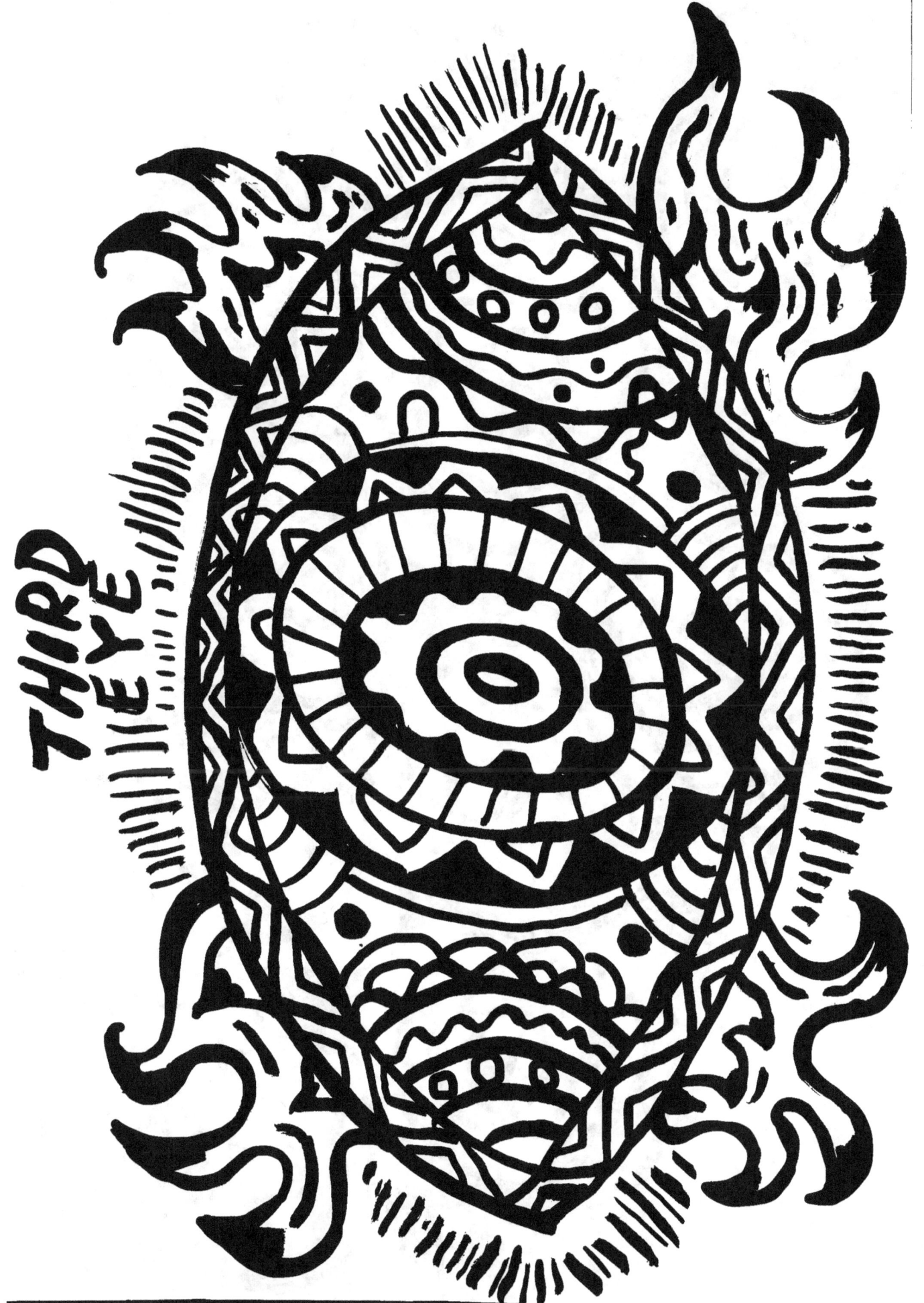

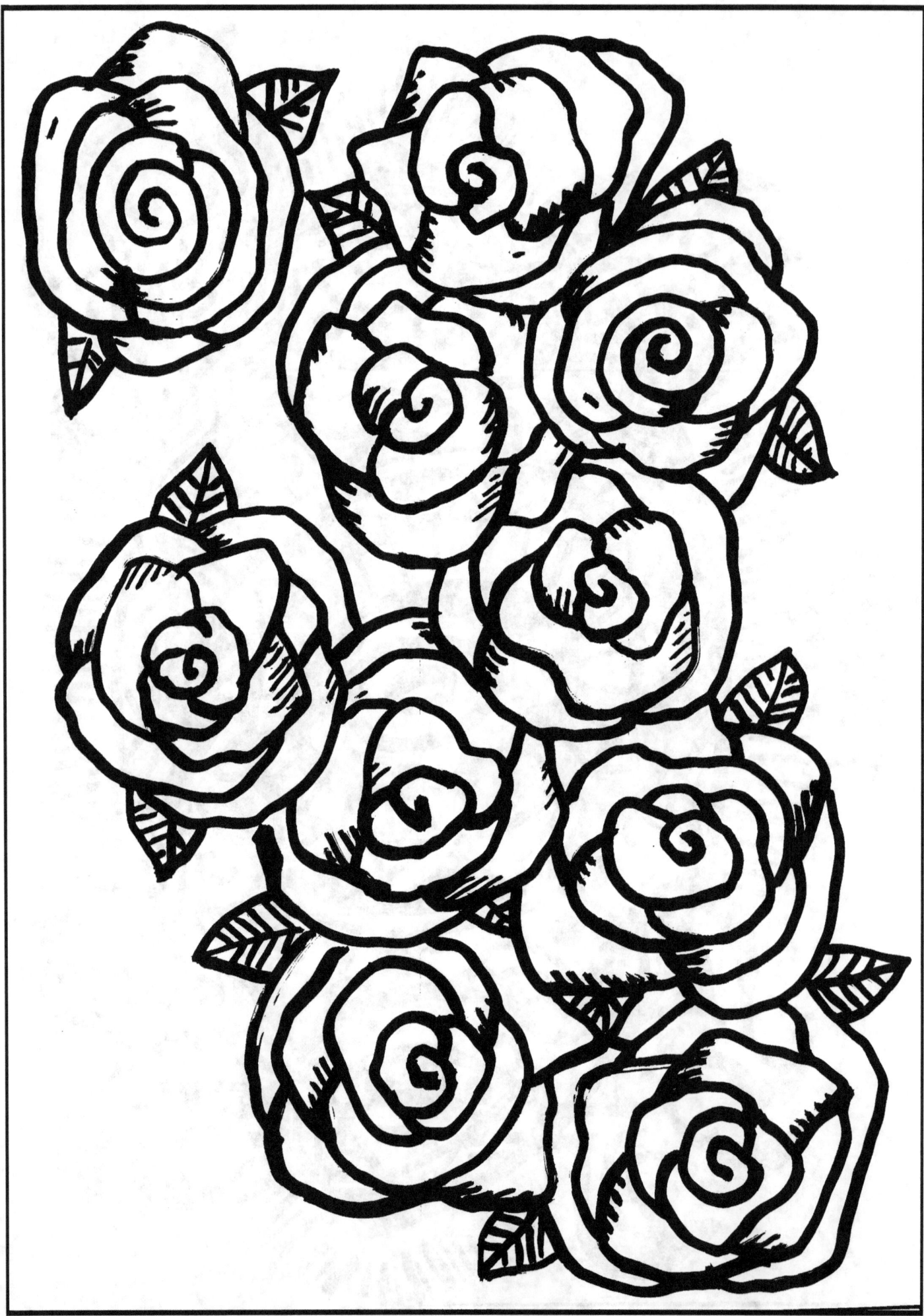

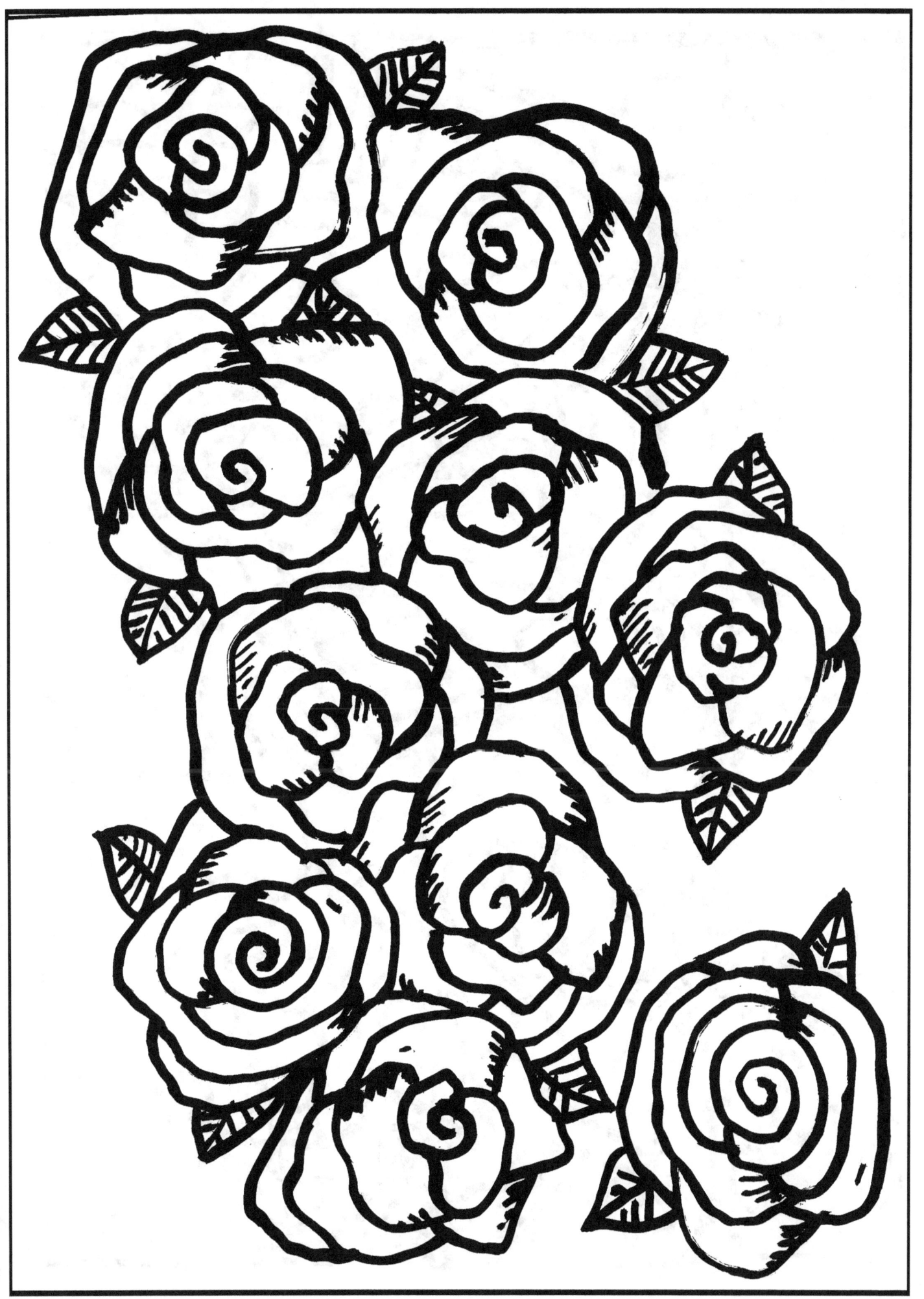

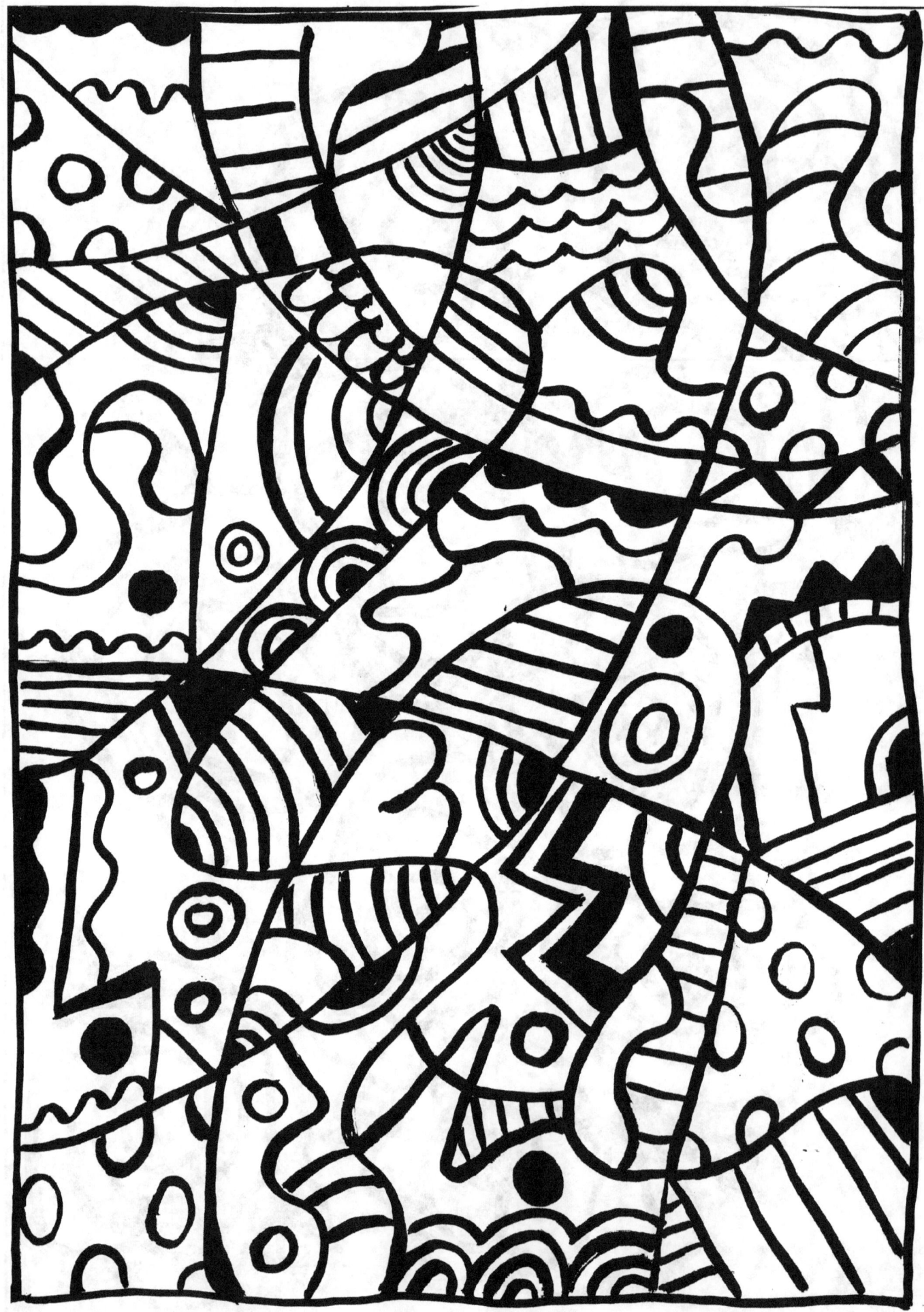

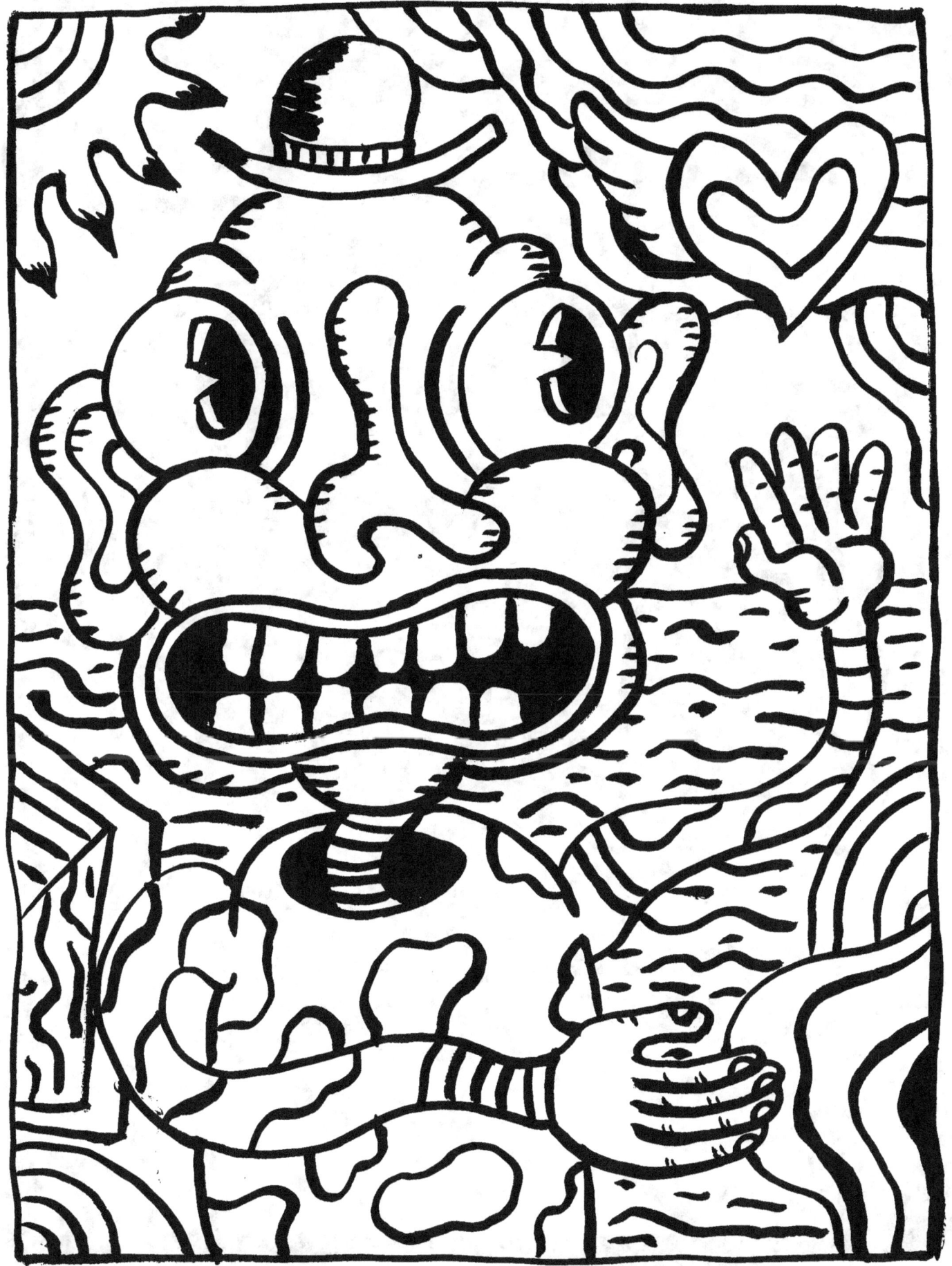

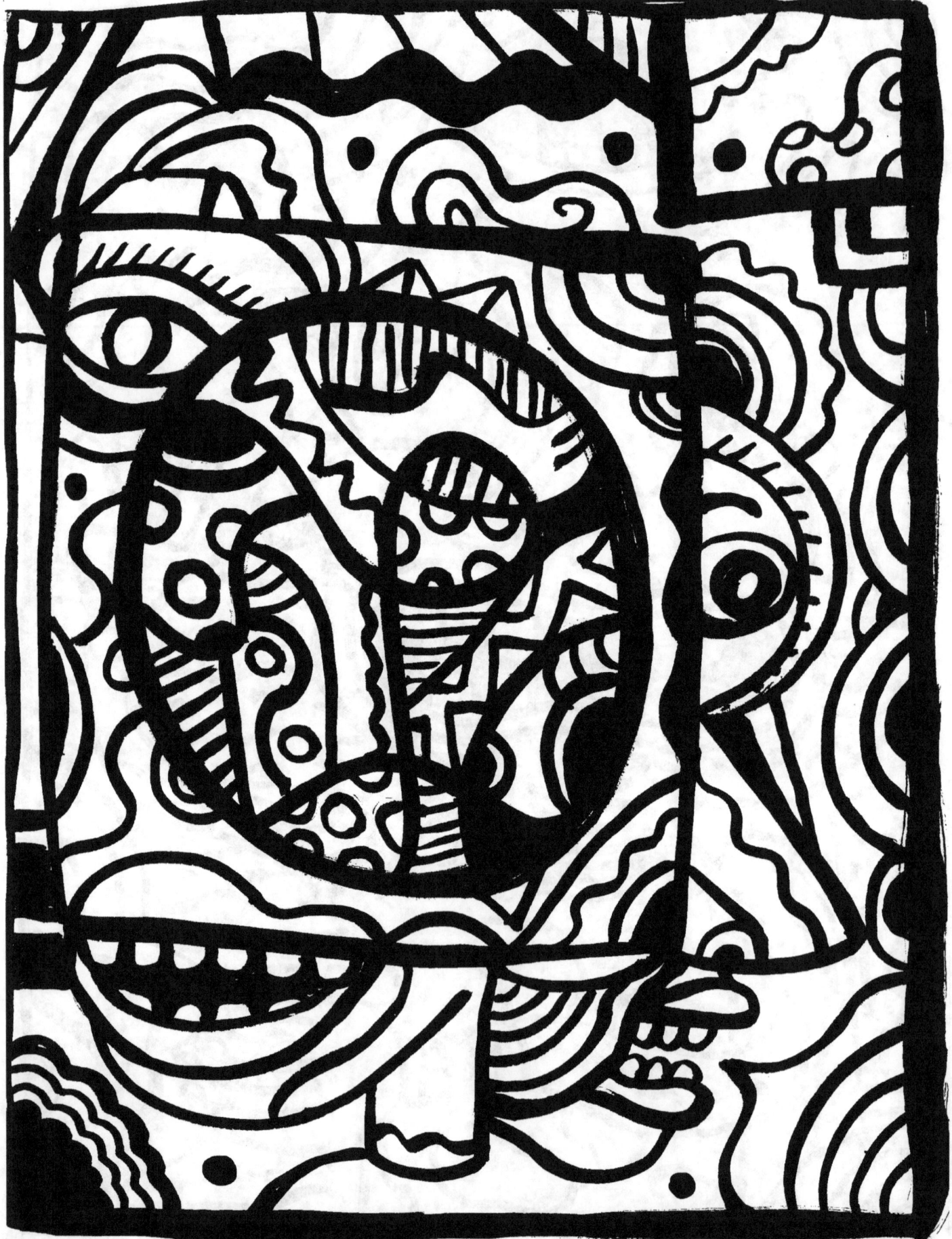

1.

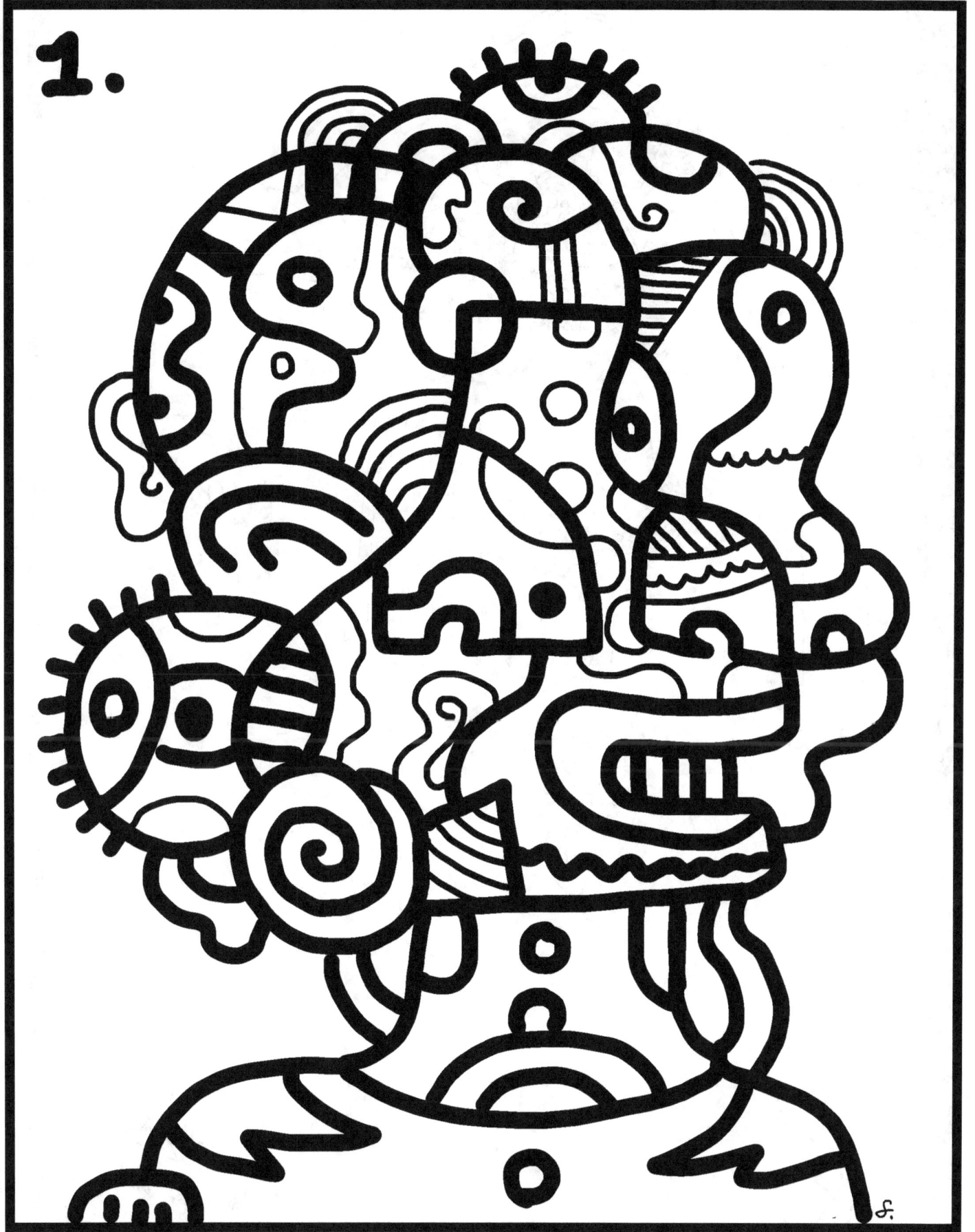

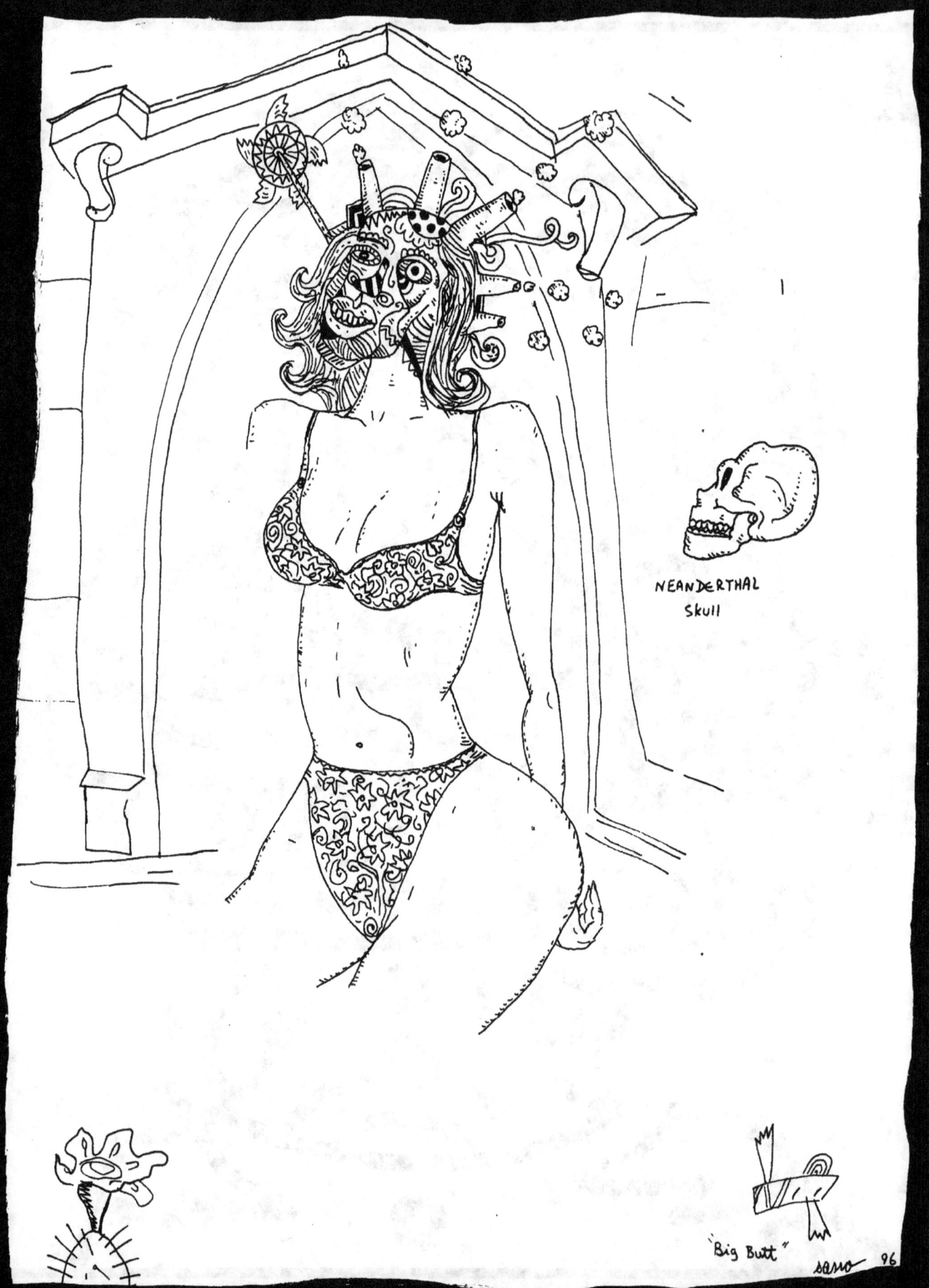

NEANDERTHAL
Skull

"Big Butt"

sasso   96

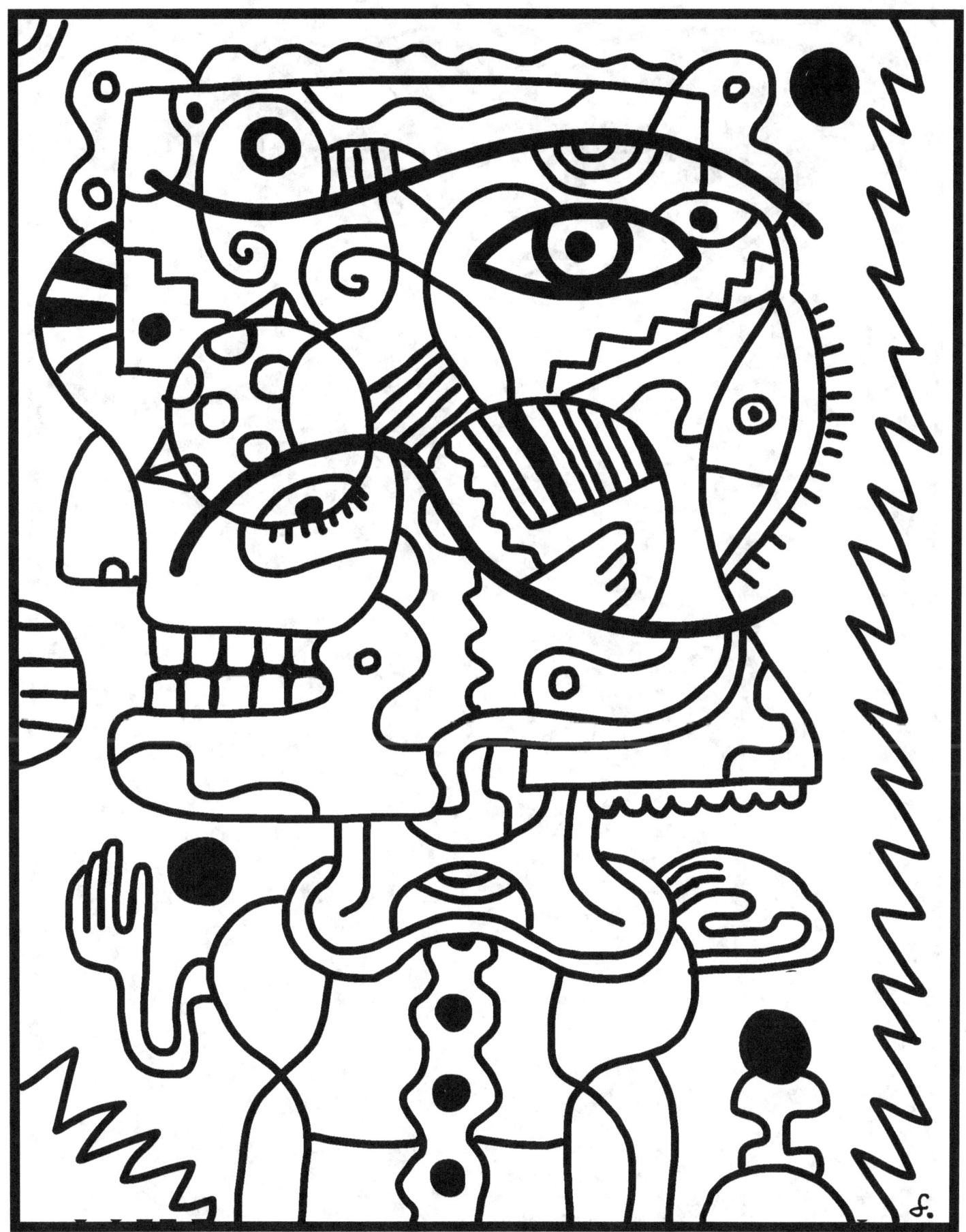

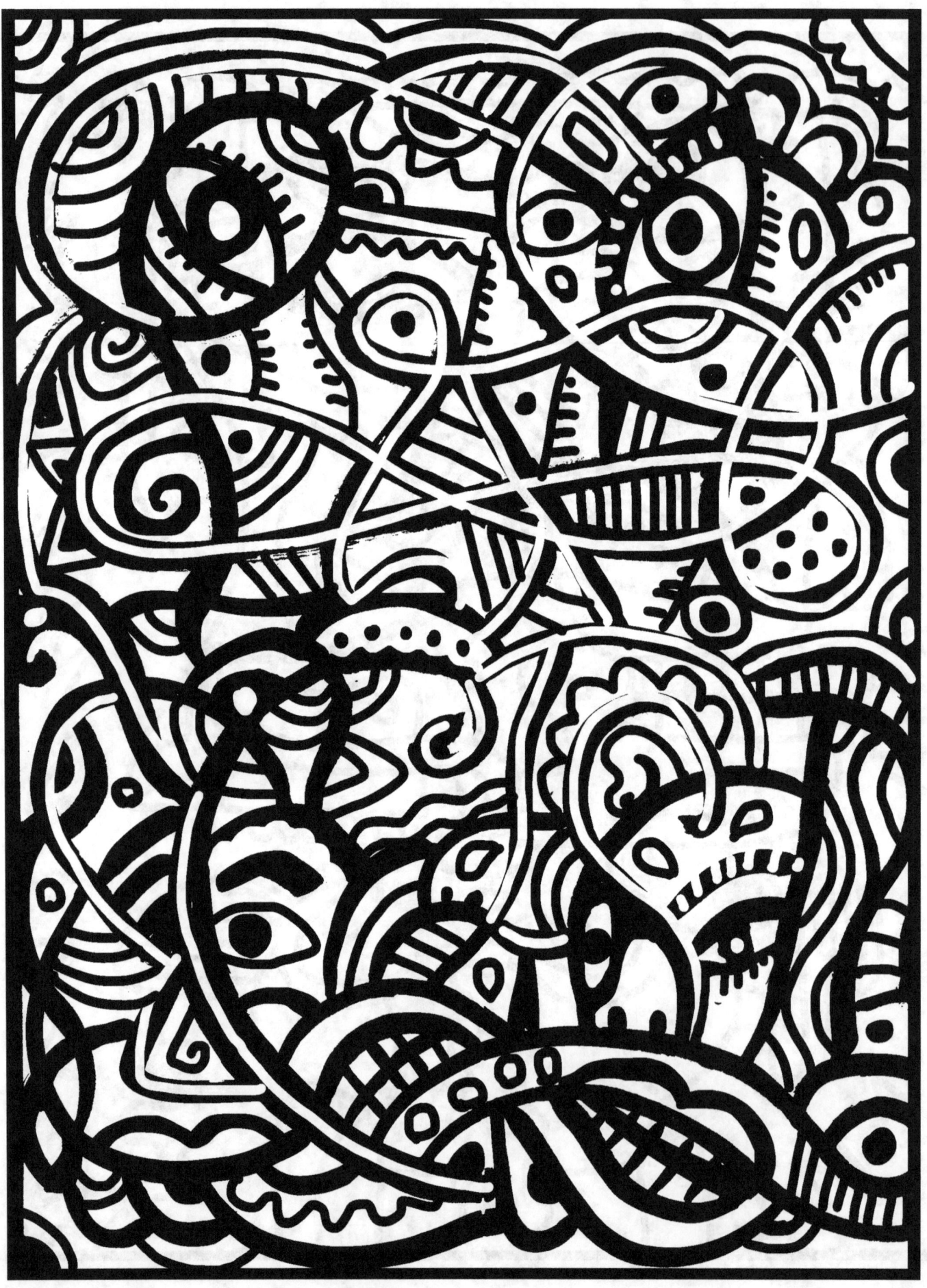

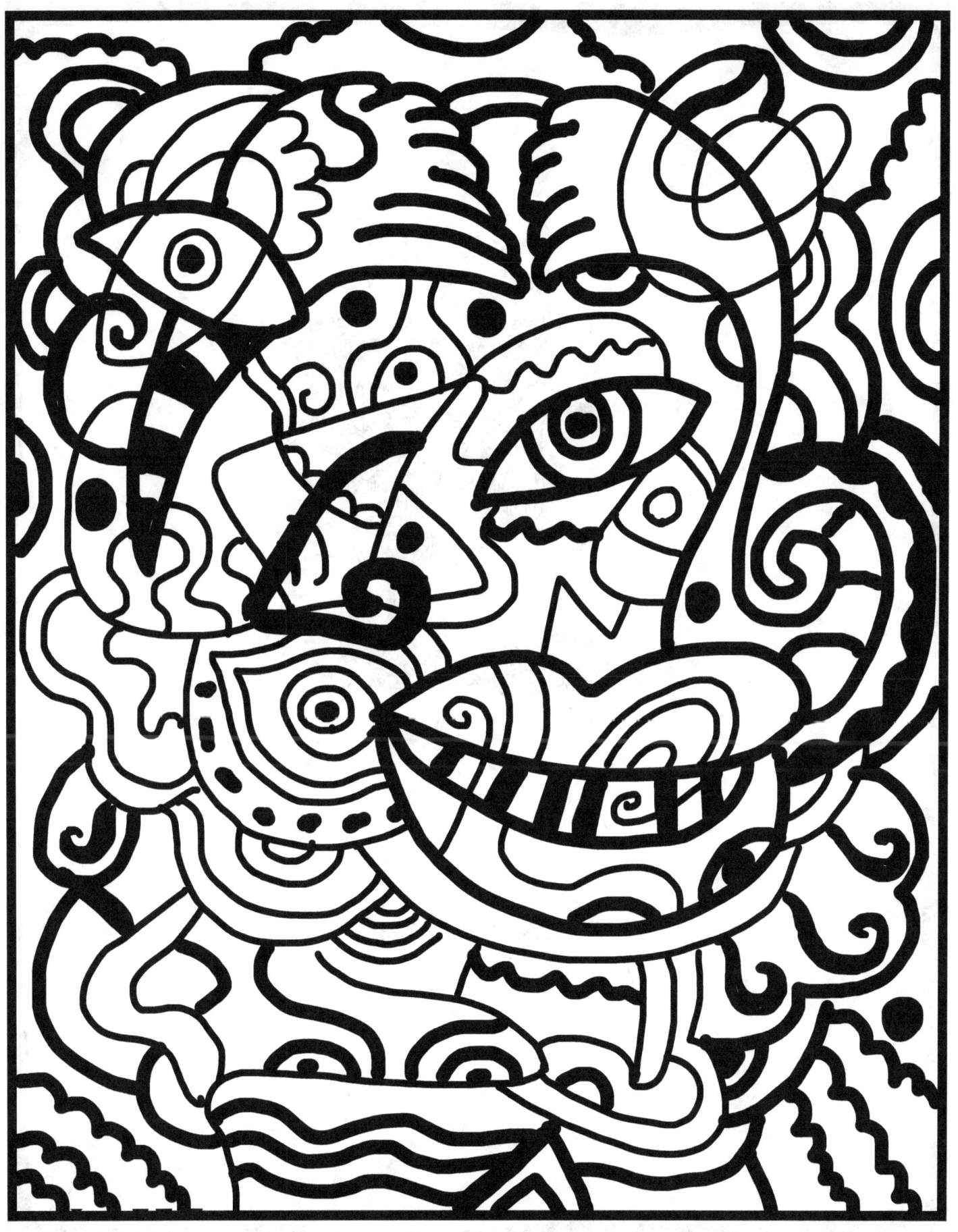

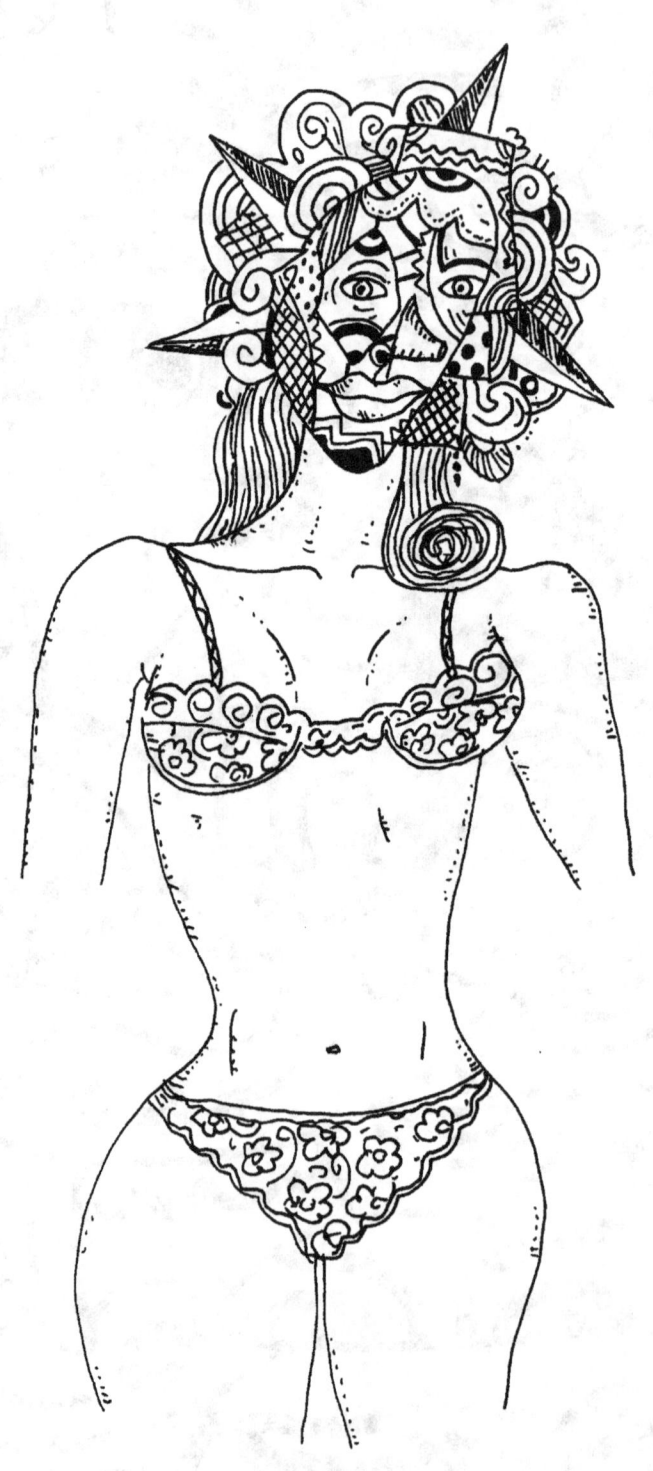

BAUBLE
1996

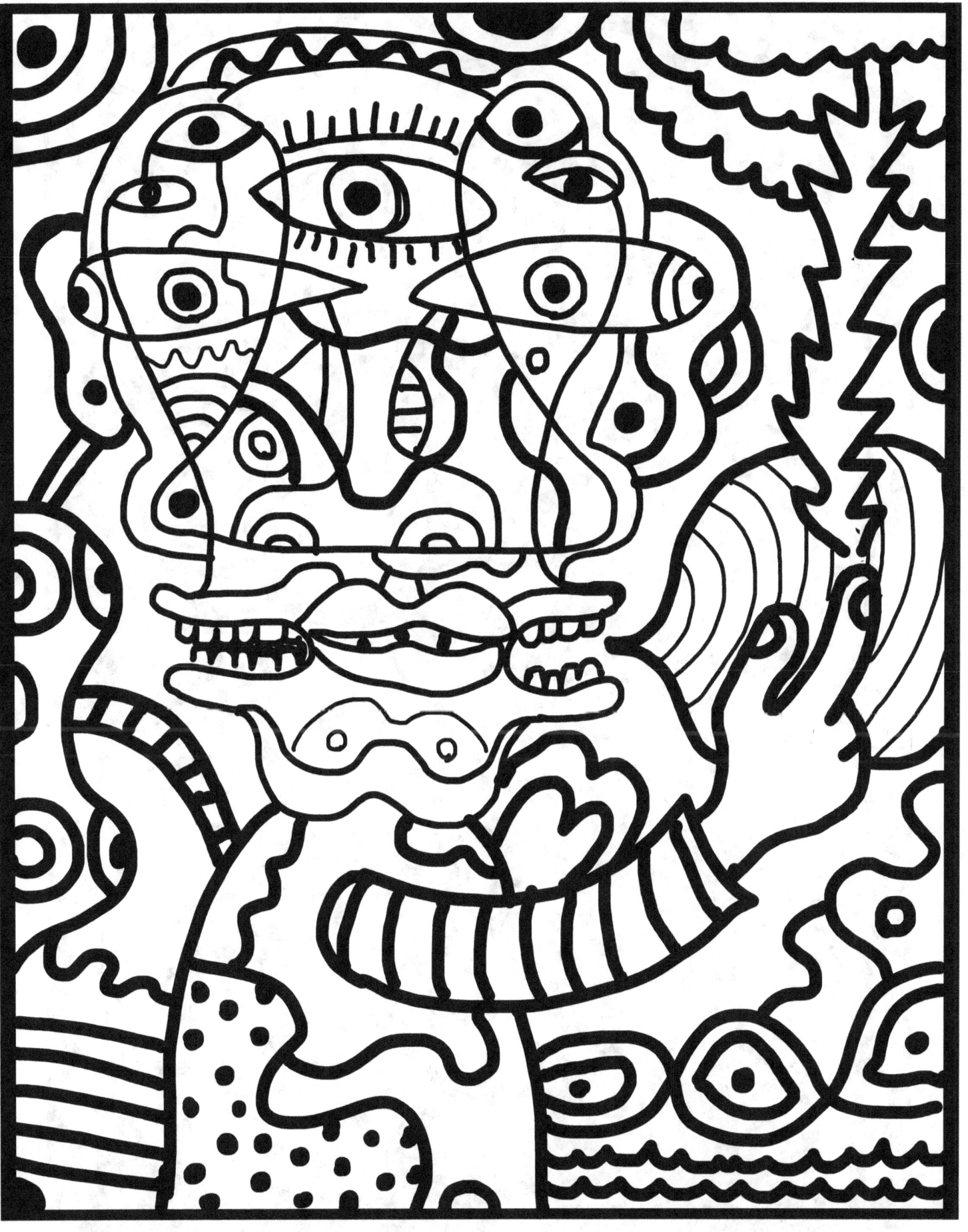

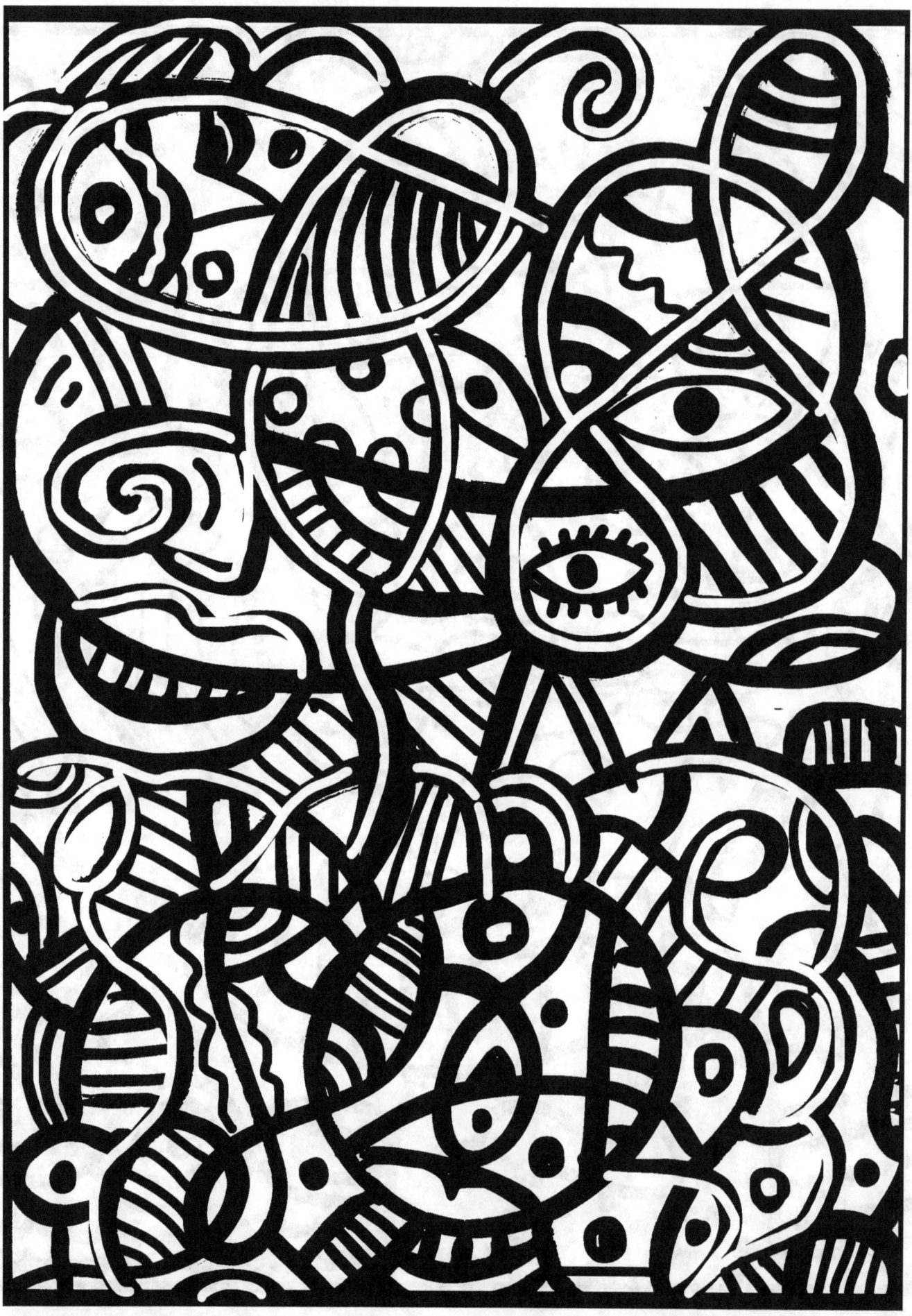

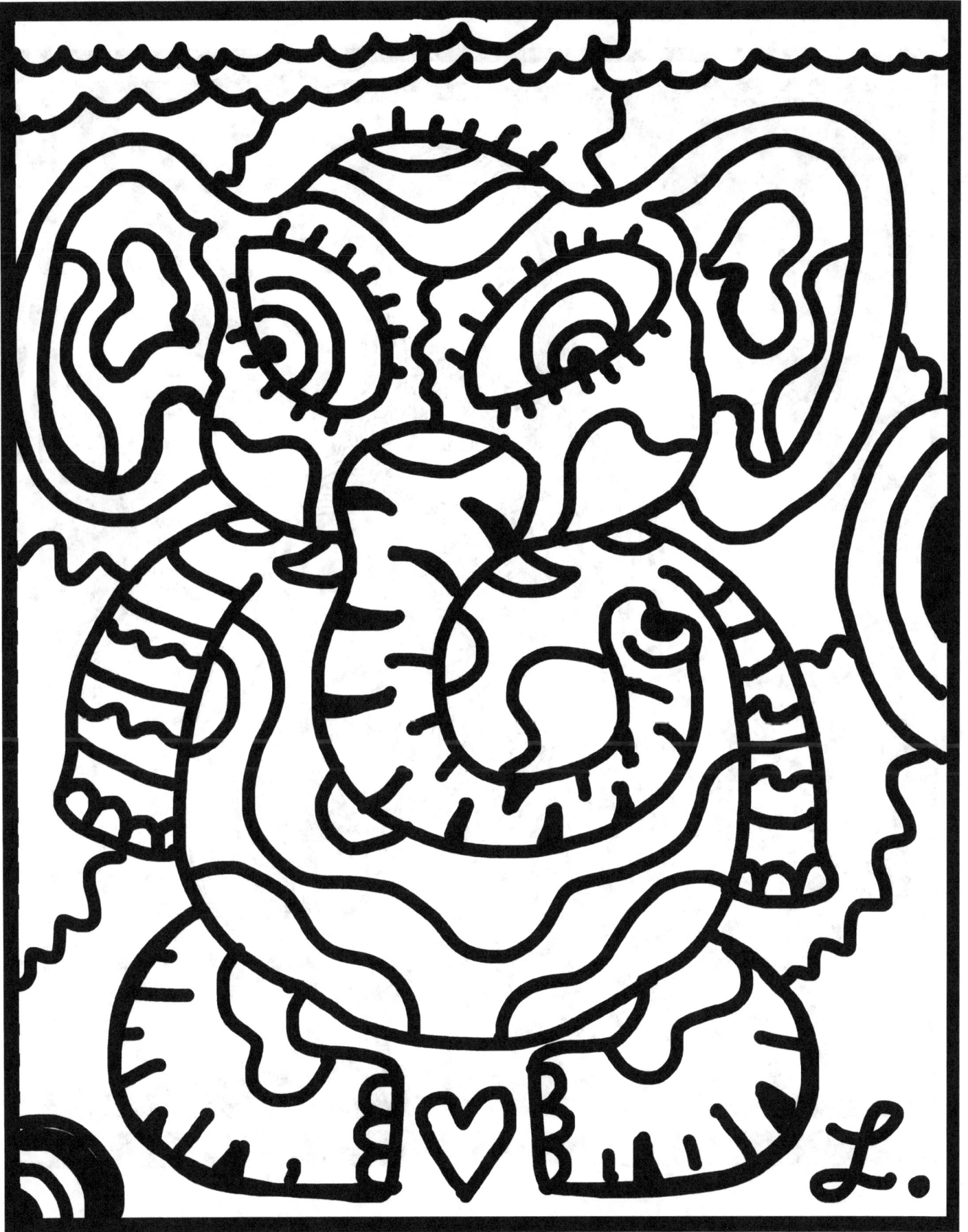

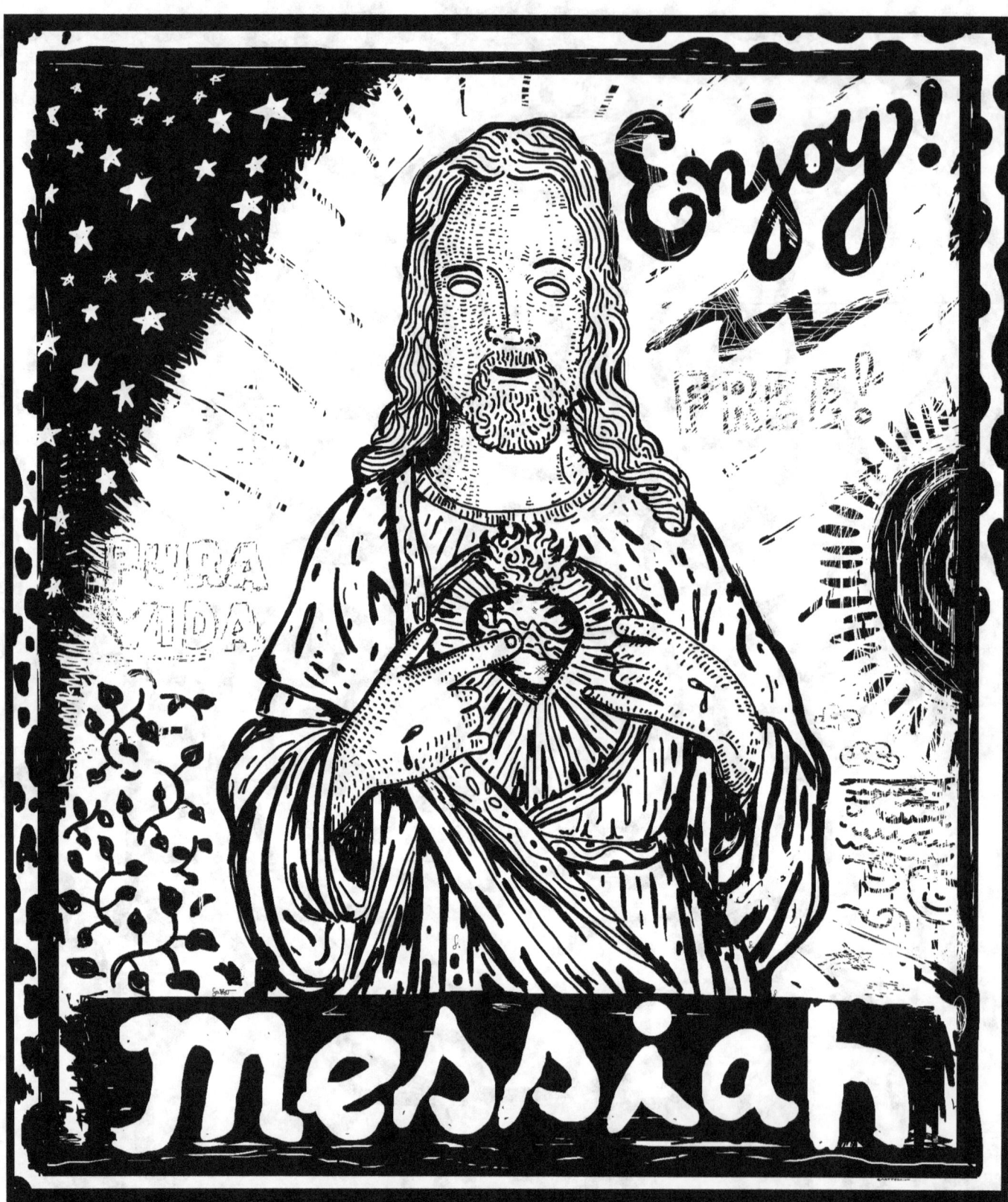

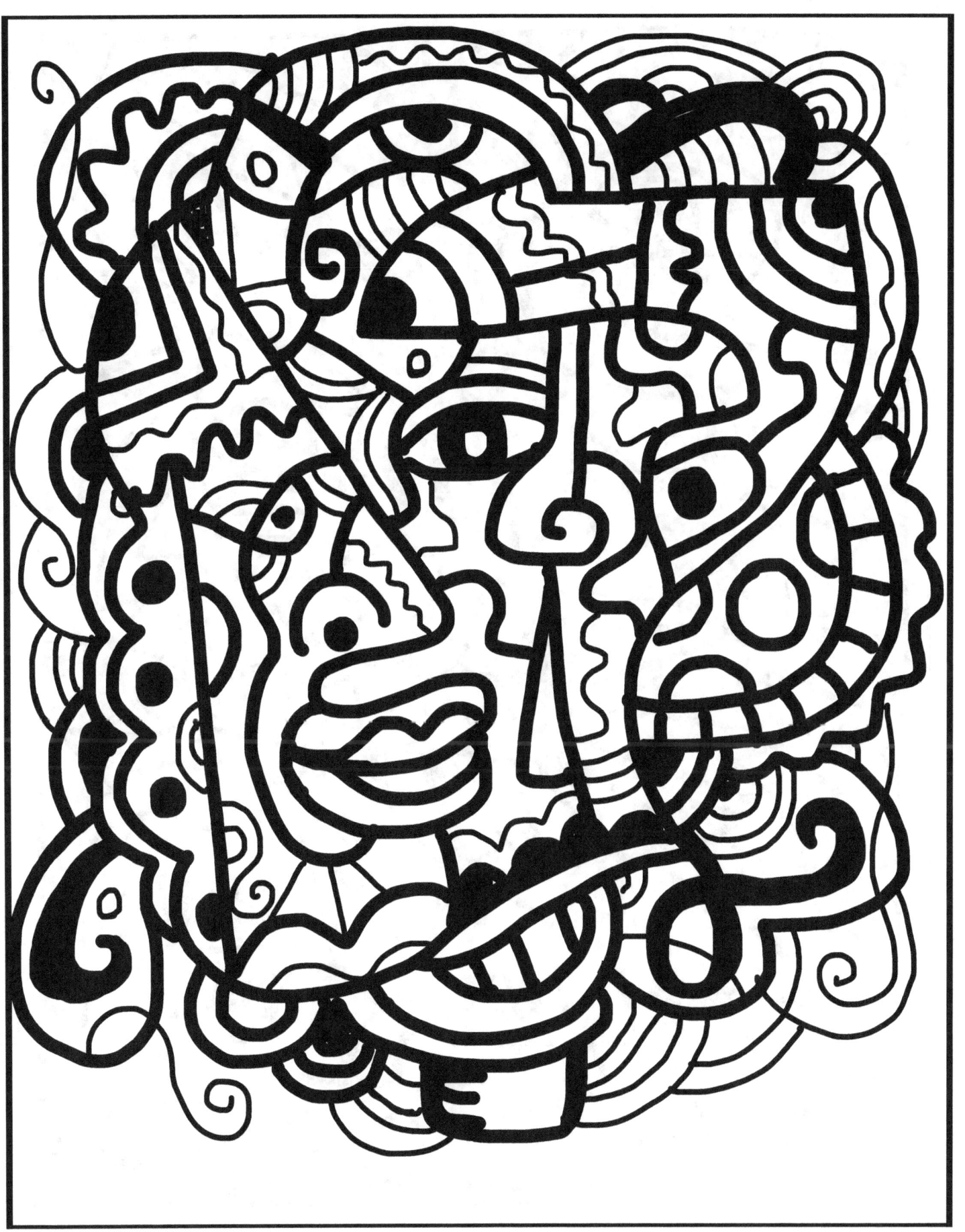

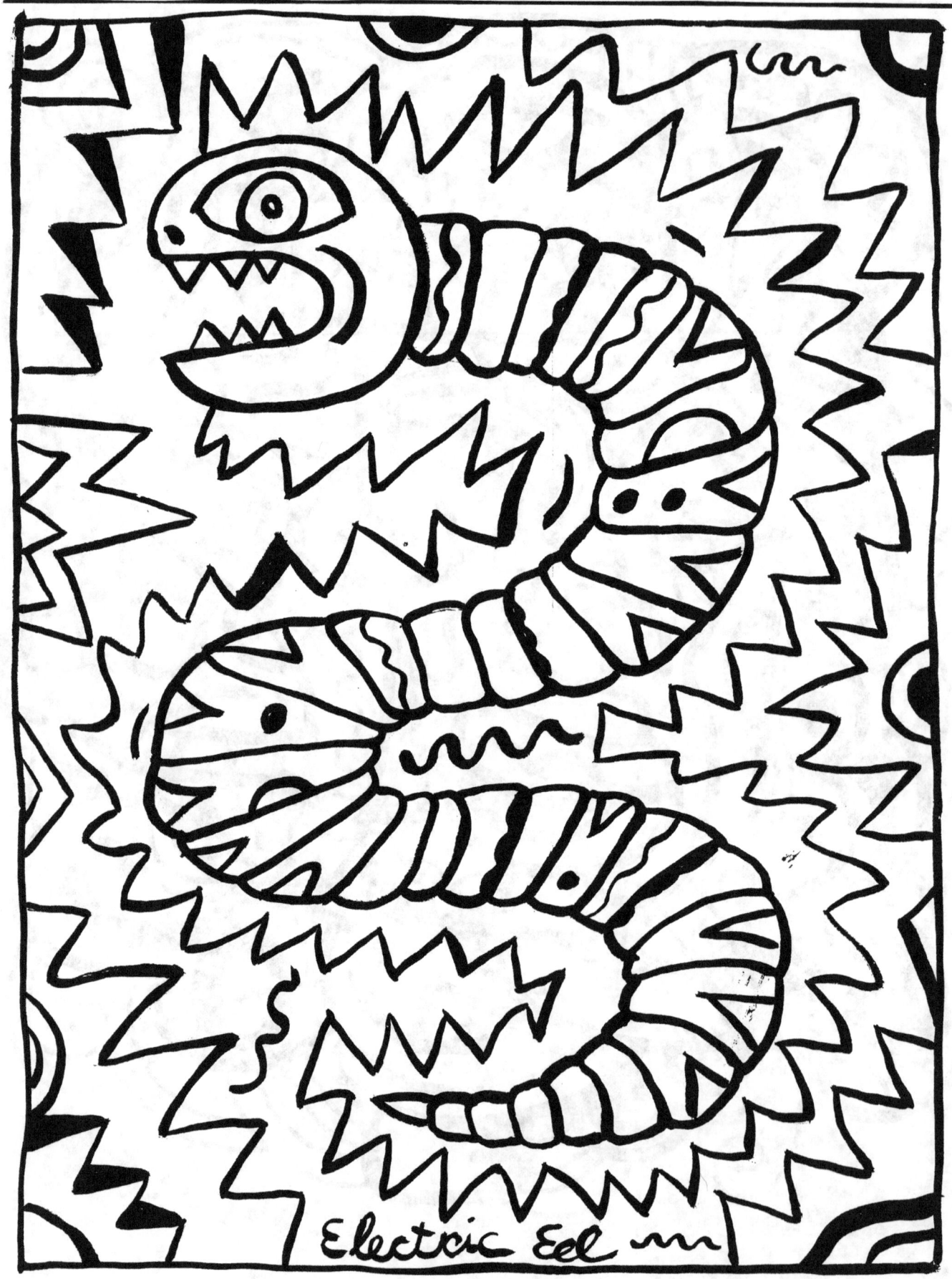

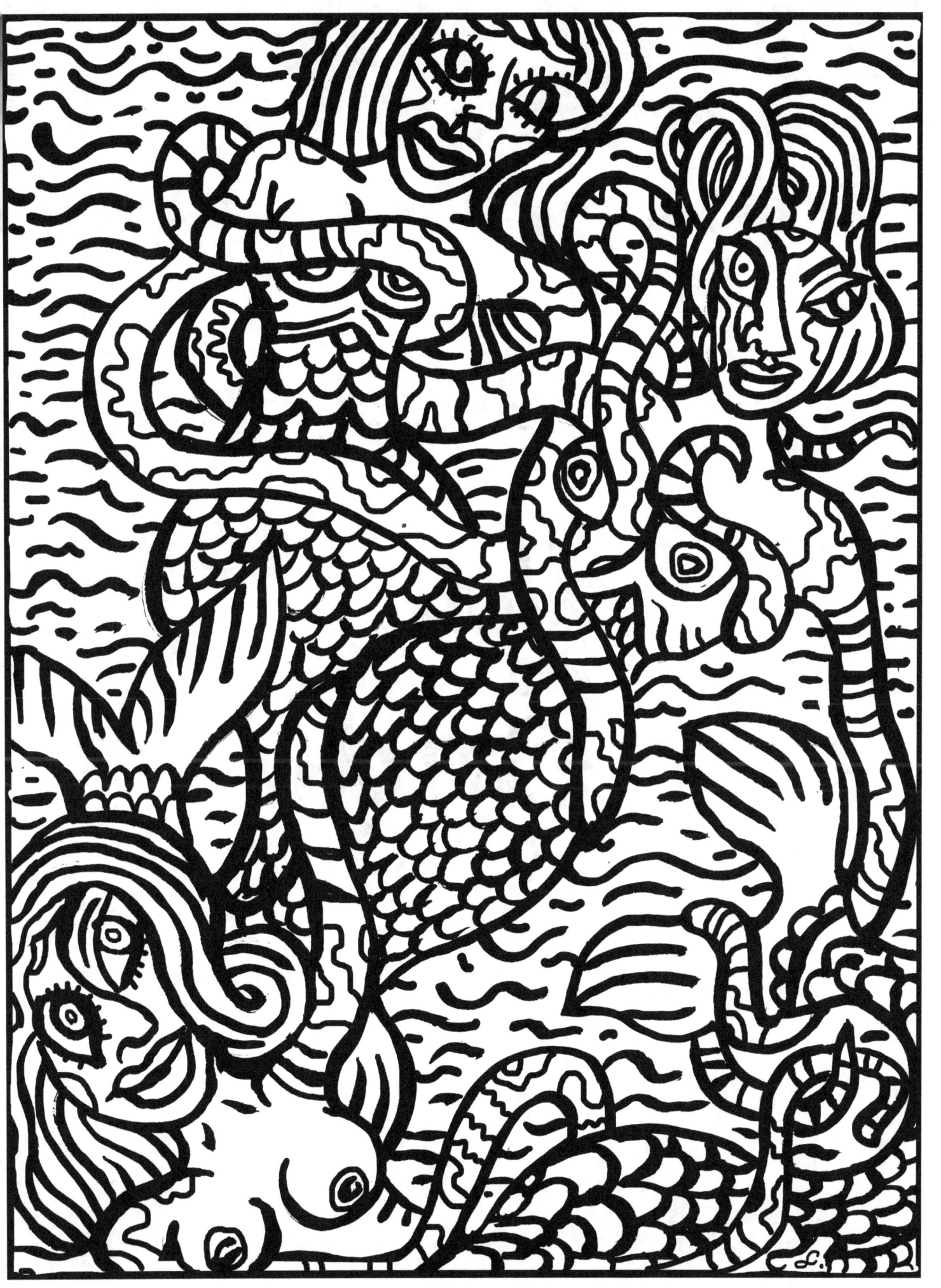

THE POOR MAN'S PICASSO
A collection of ink drawings and coloring book

the
End

www.ingramcontent.com/pod-product-compliance
Lightning Source LLC
Chambersburg PA
CBHW080820180526
45168CB00006B/2517